LISTOWEL AND ITS VICINITY
SINCE 1973

D1265330

*The more one researches the history of Listowel and its vicinity
the more one becomes aware of the goodness and kindness
the people of the area have experienced from
the Presentation Sisters,
so I dedicate this book to
the sisters who have
served and are serving
at Listowel and Lixnaw.*

LISTOWEL

and its vicinity

Since 1973

J. Anthony Gaughan

CURRACH
PRESS

First published in 2004 by
CURRACH PRESS
55A Spruce Avenue, Stillorgan Industrial Park, Blackrock, Co Dublin

www.currach.ie

Cover design by Currach Press
Cover illustrations by Olive Stack
Origination by Currach Press
Printed in Ireland by Betaprint Ltd, Dublin

ISBN 1-85607-912-0

ACKNOWLEDGEMENTS

In connection with the preparation of this book I wish to thank the staff of the National Library of Ireland, especially Dónal Ó Luanaigh, and the staff of the County Library, Tralee, County Kerry, particularly Michael Costello, for their courtesy and help. I am grateful to the custodians of the institutions listed on p.175 for allowing me to consult files and records in their charge. My thanks are also due to all who gave me information: officers of the civic organisations described on pp.35-8 , the writers or relatives of writers included in Chapters 6 and 7, the artists profiled in Chapter 8 and those whose names appear on pp.177-9. In this regard Sr Consolata Bracken, Vincent Carmody, Michael Dowling, Sr Margaret Flynn, Francis (Frank) Hayes, Mary McGillicuddy, John Molyneaux, Fr Patrick (Pat) Moore, Joseph (Joe) Murphy, Chriss Nolan, Michelle O'Donnell, John O'Flaherty, Oliver O'Neill, Justine O'Shea, Edward (Ned) O'Sullivan, Patrick (Patsy) O'Sullivan, Leslie (Les) Tervit, Cara Trant and William (Willie) Wixted have been particularly helpful.

I feel honoured in having the foreword provided by Maurice O'Connell.

I am indebted to Stephen Collins, Canon Patrick J.

Horgan and Maurice O'Connell for helpful criticisms.

I am grateful to Eileen Francis for preparing the manuscript for publication and to Brian Lynch for the design and layout of the book.

I am delighted to have the book published by Currach Press.

Finally, I wish to acknowledge with gratitude a grant from Kerry Group plc towards the publication of this work.

J. Anthony Gaughan
Newtownpark Avenue
Blackrock
County Dublin
1 May 2004

CONTENTS

LIST OF ILLUSTRATIONS

1. Ballinclemesig Gold Box, late Bronze Age 700–800 BC (photo: National Museum of Ireland)
2. Parish Pastoral Council 2002–2003 (photo: Brendan Landy)
3. Urban District Council 1979–1985 (photo: Kevin Coleman)
4. Executive Directors of Kerry Group plc 2004 (photo: Kerry Group plc)
5. Presentation Sisters 1994 (photo: Brendan Landy)
6. Gabriel Fitzmaurice with Fr J. Anthony Gaughan and Bryan MacMahon 1984 (photo: Kieran Moloney)
7. Professor Máire Herbert 2003
8. Katie Hannon, author and journalist, 2004 (photo: Brendan Landy)
9. The Celtic festival of spring in copper by Tony O'Callaghan, commissioned by the Central Bank of Ireland in 1979 (photo: Lensmen)
10. Members of the Listowel branch of Comhaltas Ceoltóirí Éireann in the old market yard before setting out 'on the wren' to raise funds for the Old Folks Home, St Stephen's Day 1968
11. Daniel (Danny) Hannon with members of the Lartigue Theatre Company 2004 (photo: Brendan Landy)

FOREWORD

More than thirty years have passed since *Listowel and its vicinity* was published. It was a masterpiece of local history, covering varied aspects of life and times in North Kerry from the beginnings of organised society to modern times. The book quickly became a collector's item and today copies are highly prized.

The pace of change in the past thirty years has been quite extraordinary by all previous experience. Listowel continues to prosper. The population of the town has risen. The town is brighter and livelier than before and there is a sense of affluence about the place. The hinterland is also flourishing due, among other things, to the impact of the European Union on the farming community. Employment opportunities have exceeded the best expectations. Kerry Group plc, which started life in the Canon's field in 1972, has now become a major player in the global food business.

Some things never change. Access to primary and secondary education continues to be a top priority. The interest in literary endeavour is as vibrant as ever and new names continue to come forward to replace those who have sadly passed away. The opening of the Kerry Literary and Cultural Centre in September 2000 was a landmark development in preserving the cultural traditions of North Kerry. Gaelic football continues to be the most popular game in the area. Even the Lartigue railway has made a kind of comeback with some ambitious plans still in the pipeline.

This supplement will be of special interest to those who are fortunate to possess copies of the original *Listowel and its vicinity*. It will command attention for all who are interested in local history as a pen-picture of the evolution of a society in the course of one generation. As always, Father J. Anthony Gaughan is meticulous and comprehensive in his research. This has been a hallmark in all his writing over many years.

Maurice O'Connell
24 March 2004

ANTIQUARIAN AND ARCHAEOLOGICAL ACTIVITY

There has been considerable activity in North Kerry of interest to antiquarians and archaeologists since 1973. Much of this was carried out under the aegis of the North Kerry Archaeological Committee. Established in 1986, it enabled AnCO to publish in 1988 *Streets of Listowel* which included pictures of the most attractive shop fronts in the town. It facilitated the publication in 1990 of Gráinne O'Connell and Bernadette Tarrant's *Exploring the rich heritage of the North Kerry Landscape*, an illustrated thesaurus of the area's history, folklore, legends, sacred sites and archaeology. Its crowning achievement was the publication in 1995 of Caroline Toal's *North Kerry Archaeological Survey*.

The work of the North Kerry Archaeological Committee was complemented by the Rattoo Heritage Society. Founded in 1988, it established the North Kerry Museum in 1990. Situated in Knoppóge, near Ballyduff, this has numerous artefacts, including prehistoric fossils and an ancient log ferry-boat. But, essentially, it is a folk museum with an interesting collection of farm and household implements, including a number of quernstones which had been used in the area in the eighteenth and nineteenth centuries. Apart from establishing the museum, the Rattoo Heritage Society has also produced a number of video-films on the history of North Kerry.[1]

Earlier, in 1973, Dermot C. Twohig conducted an excavation at Dromkeen East, Causeway. In his report[2] he described the site as an univallate (one bank and ditch) ring-fort within which there was a *souterrain* complex, consisting of a beehive chamber, whence there were three exits. Nearby, he also excavated a Fulacht Fiadh (an ancient cooking site from the bronze age).[3] This consisted of a horseshoe-shaped mound of burnt stone intermixed with finely-ground charcoal. The excavation showed that the cooking trough was set into the floor of a large pit, cut into the field surface.

In his survey in 1995[4] of the promontory forts of the Kerry peninsula, Markus Redmond included two sited at the top of Kerry Head. He described the surviving defences of Tiduff/An Tigh Duibh – Cathair Cairbre Mór and those of the fort of the same name nearby.

In 2001 Florence M. Hurley conducted a small archaeological excavation in the interior of Listowel castle on behalf of Dúchas, the heritage service. This was in advance of conservation work on the site which included the refurbishment of the front of the castle and the repair of the central stairway to the roof. The excavation revealed considerable disturbance related to the demolition of the bulk of the castle in the eighteenth and nineteenth centuries. Part of the foundation trench of the west wall of

---

1. Information from Seán Quinlan.
2. Dermot C. Twohig, 'Excavation at Dromkeen East, Causeway', *K.A.H.S.J.* 7 (1974) pp.5–10.
3. Ibid., p.11, Dermot C. Twohig, 'Excavation of a Fulacht Fiadh at Dromkeen East, Causeway', *K.A.H.S.J.* 10 (1977) pp.5–13.
4. Markus Redmond, 'A Survey of the promontory forts of the Kerry peninsulas', *K.A.H.S.J.* 28 (1995) pp.5–63.

the castle was found. All the finds were post–medieval or modern in date.[5]

In 1996 work on the layout of the Square led to the discovery of a neatly-constructed, stone-lined well. Now known as the 'Writers Well', this is situated near the rear of St John's Theatre and Arts Centre. However, no reference to its origin seems to have survived.

During the past thirty years a number of finds have been reported to the authorities in the National Museum. A small number of these were significant.

Ballinclemesig Gold Box

In 1975 a small gold box from the late bronze age 700–800 BC was discovered at Ballinclemesig, Ballyheigue. It was subsequently acquired by the National Museum.[6]

In 1978, 1979 and 1983 artefacts variously described as a log boat, a dugout wooden boat and a dugout canoe were discovered in the Cashen River. The first of these was reported on by Eamonn P. Kelly,[7] and the other two by Patrick Healy.[8] In 1979, a wooden container of butter was found in the bog at Banemore. This was also examined and surveyed by Patrick Healy.[9] In 1977 an ancient road was

---

5. For more, see National Museum of Ireland 98 E 0293.

6. Michael Ryan, 'A gold box from Ballinclemesig,' *K.A.H.S.J.* 14 (1981) pp.5-9; N.M.I. 1975/256. For more, see Mary Cahill, 'The end of a mystery – how the gold "box" from Ballinclemesig was used', *Kerry Magazine* 14 (2003) pp.10-11.

7. Eamonn P. Kelly, 'A log boat from Derryco', *K.A.H.S.J.* 14 (1981) pp.10-13.

8. Patrick Healy, 'Dugout wooden boat in the estuary of the Cashen', *K.A.H.S.J.* 14 (1981) pp.115-16; *Kerryman* 16 September 1983; N.M.I. 1A/127/83.

9. Patrick Healy, 'Container of butter from a bog at Banemore', *K.A.H.S.J.* 14 (1981) pp.112-15.

discovered in the bog at Islandanny, Duagh.[10]

In 1974 Michael Dolley published an extended note[11] on a hoard of 'gun–money' which had been discovered at Dromkeen West, Causeway, in 1961. The money was known as 'gun–money' because the coins were struck in metal obtained from melting down obsolete cannon. They were minted for James II and dated March 1689 and March 1690.

---

10. N.M.I., 1A/3/77.

11. Michael Dolley, 'A hoard of the so-called "gun-money" from Causeway', *K.A.H.S.J.* 7 (1974) pp.146-8.

PARISH

Catholic

After 1973 Listowel Catholic parish continued to be a union of the civil parishes of Listowel, Finuge, more than half of Galey and a small portion of Dysert. Its staff remained a parish priest and two curates, all of whom continued to reside in the presbytery adjacent to St Mary's church. Mgr James Sheahan was parish priest from 1973 until he died in 1985. A native of Beale, he had previously been administrator of Killarney parish from 1960 to 1973. While in Listowel he responded to an appeal for help in the African missions and served as parish priest in Nakuru in Kenya, from 1975 to 1977.

Mgr Sheahan was succeeded by Mgr Michael Leahy in 1986. A native of Knockanure, he had been parish priest of Allihies from 1975 to 1976 and of Tarbert from 1976 to 1986. He retired in 1996. Canon James Linnane was appointed to Listowel in 1996. He had previously been president of St Brendan's Seminary, Killarney, from 1981 to 1985, president of St Michael's College from 1985 to 1989 and parish priest of Duagh from 1989 to 1996.

During the past thirty-one years the number of

parishioners has risen *pari passu* with the increase in the population of Listowel's urban and rural districts. Population figures for these in 1971 were: Listowel Urban District 3,010; Listowel Rural District 1,129. These figures had risen to 3,569 and 1,208 in 2002. The population of the rest of the rural complement of the parish, for the most part, remained unchanged at about 1,200. Thus, while the parishioners of Listowel numbered some 5,329 in 1971, they numbered just under 6,000 in 2002. Apart from providing divine worship, the sacraments and the rites of passage, the clergy have pastoral responsibility for five nursing homes, four primary schools, a special needs school and three post-primary schools. Their pastoral ministry is complemented by those involved in lay ministries and the traditional lay Catholic organisations.

Following a directive from Bishop William (Bill) Murphy, a Parish Pastoral Council was set up in October 2000. Patrick (Patsy) O'Sullivan was elected chairman. The Council issued the following mission statement: 'To promote and develop reflection and prayer, worship of God and care of others. This to happen in a vibrant, supportive and truly Christian community, where everybody feels welcome, secure and valued.' The Council's monthly meetings during the following three years included prayer and a wide-ranging discussion of the pastoral and other needs of the parish with a view to increasing the effectiveness of the various groups dealing with them. O'Sullivan was re-elected chairman of the Council in 2003.

As elsewhere in the Catholic world the Second Vatican Council 1962-5 had a significant influence on the devotional life of Listowel and the other parishes in North Kerry. The introduction of the vernacular into the liturgy and the emphasis on Bible-based services led to a general erosion of support for hitherto popular and traditional devotions. Eventually, by the end of the century, benediction, the rosary, novenas, parish missions and retreats had little support. The disagreements among parishioners on the merits and demerits of these developments became evident in 1977 when the sanctuary of St Mary's church was re-ordered to conform to the liturgical norms of the General Council. Some committed parishioners mounted a strong protest which was as much motivated by their disillusionment with changes in devotional practice as a determination to see that the artistic integrity of the church was not jeopardised.[1] A further and less controversial renovation of St Mary's was completed in 2001.

By far the most profound change in the devotional practice of the people of Listowel and the other parishes of North Kerry occurred from about the mid-1980s onwards. For the previous one hundred and fifty years the deep Catholic faith of people in this area was evidenced, particularly in the last century, not least by their regular attendance at Sunday Mass and the high incidence of vocations to the priesthood and the religious life. By the beginning of the new millennium these were no longer features of Listowel and its vicinity. A large minority were no longer regular Mass-goers and there had been a serious decline in vocations to the priesthood and religious life. Yet, notwithstanding the increasing secularisation of Irish society, Christian traditions, standards and values continued to be respected in the area.[2]

1. See *Kerryman* 4 March 1977.
2. Information from Fr George Hayes, Kerry diocesan secretary; Canon James Linnane, P.P., and Patrick O'Sullivan, chairman, Listowel Parish Pastoral Council.

Church of Ireland

Owing to the decrease in numbers of members of the Church of Ireland and Protestants generally in North Kerry, there was a radical re-organisation of the Church's parishes in this area. The union of Kilnaughtin, Listowel and Ballybunion continued until Archdeacon John Murdock Wallace retired in 1982. These parishes were then added to the Tralee union and became the responsibility of Archdeacon R.W.P. Doherty. In 1988 he was succeeded by Canon Robert Warren, whose group of parishes was listed as: Tralee S[t] John E[vangelist], Ballymacelligott, Ballyseedy and Kilnaughtin (Tarbert) S[t] Brendan.

In 1994 Kilnaughtin, the parish effectively representing the North Kerry area, was transferred to the incumbent of the Rathkeale, County Limerick, union of parishes. The incumbent of that union was Reverend R.G. Graham until 1997 when he was succeeded by Reverend S.E. Mourant. The latter served until 2000, after which no appointment was made to the union.[3]

---

3. *Church of Ireland Directories* 1973-2003.

APPENDIX 1

Priests from Listowel Parish 1973–2003				
Name	**Townland of origin**	**Colleges attended**	**Year of ordination**	**Diocese**
Hayes, George	Gortnaminsha	St Michael's and Maynooth	1993	Kerry
O'Shea, Richard	Listowel	St Michael's and Maynooth	1988	Kerry
Tarrant, Joseph	Listowel	St Michael's and Maynooth	1986	Kerry

TOWN

Local Government Administration

Prior to 1898 local government administration was fragmented across a number of authorities. These were: Grand Juries, Boards of Guardians and in certain towns, Town Commissioners. The Commissioners were established in Listowel after 1854 and the town became an Urban Sanitary District in 1883.

The Local Government (Ireland) Act 1898 simplified the local government system. It provided for the setting up of elective councils for the management of county, district and municipal affairs, with a uniform electorate throughout Ireland for the election of these councils. Thereby Grand Juries were deprived of their fiscal functions and Boards of Guardians lost their rating powers, their expenditure in future being provided for by grants made by the county councils, borough councils and urban district councils. In towns, such as Listowel, which were Urban Sanitary Districts the Town Commissioners were replaced by Urban District Councils.

Under the Local Government (Ireland) Act 1919 proportional representation (single transferable vote) was to be used in municipal elections. The Local Government (Extension of Franchise) Act of 1935 gave a vote in local elections to every Irish citizen over twenty-one who was not subject to legal incapacity. Previously a thirty-year qualification was required for women to vote in local elections. Later, under the Local Elections Act 1953, the normal term for urban district councillors was changed from three to five years. Up to 1973 the postponement of the local elections required the passage of a bill by the Oireachtas, but the Local Elections Act 1973 enabled the appropriate minister to postpone them by order. The Local Elections (Amendment Order) 1974 eased the conditions which governed the use of postal voting in these elections. Finally, under the Local Government Act 2001, from 1 January 2002 urban district councils were re-named town councils and their chairpersons could henceforth be known as mayors or cathaoirligh. The Listowel councillors adopted the title of mayor when Tom Walsh was chairperson but Denis Stack was the first to serve a full year as mayor in 2002–3.

Listowel Urban District Council

In accordance with the Local Government Act of 1898 elections were held to Listowel Urban District Council on 16 January 1899. The electorate was 421, of whom 360 voted. Of the twenty-six candidates, twelve were elected in this order: D. Loughnane, J. Carroll (Lab.), J. O'Connor (Lab.), J. Broderick, D. J. Flavin, J. Bunyan (Lab.), W. L. Fitzgerald (Lab.), P. Hayes (Lab.), T. F. Cronin, M. Kerin (Lab.), M. O'Connor, W. A. Cronin (Lab.).

Local elections were held thereafter on 15 January 1902, 16 January 1905, 15 January 1908, 16 January 1911, 15 January 1914, 15 January 1920, 23 June 1925, 26 June 1928,

26 June 1934, 19 August 1942, 14 June 1945, 20 September 1950, 23 June 1955, 29 June 1960, 28 June 1967, 18 June 1974, 7 June 1979, 20 June 1985, 9 June 1994 and 11 June 1999. The irregular intervals between the local elections were due to the government postponing them for various reasons. The Listowel electorate was from one area, save for the elections in 1920, 1925, 1928 and 1934 when it was divided into an east and west ward. From the election of 1942 onwards the number of seats on the council was reduced from 12 to 9. The local elections were uncontested in 1928, 1934, 1942 and 1945.

Uncontested Local Elections

The uncontested election of 1928 was described in an official statement as follows:

> Since the passing of the first Local Government Act for Ireland, the position which was created in connection with the nomination of candidates for Listowel urban area is probably without parallel. Up to the closing time, Mrs Annie Gleeson, town clerk and returning officer, did not receive a single nomination.
>
> Listowel Urban Council ordinarily consists of twelve members but since the last election in 1925, through resignation, disqualification and other causes, this number dwindled to only three members, Thomas Walsh, Edward J. Gleeson and Patrick Browne.
>
> In accordance with the Act, Mrs Gleeson published a notice stating that as no candidates had been duly nominated for election, Messrs Walsh & Gleeson would be declared re-elected as members for the west ward and Mr Browne would be declared re-elected for the east ward.

The official statement issued after the 1934 election was uncontested read:

> There was no contest for the Listowel Urban District Council. This was brought about by the withdrawal of all the United Ireland Party nominations and two Fianna Fáil candidates.
>
> It was stated by Mr John Dennehy, chairman of the U.I.P. Election Committee, that his party's action in withdrawing was as a protest against the action of Mrs Annie Gleeson, returning officer, who declared two U.I.P. nominations invalid, for being incorrectly filled. He also stated that the U.I.P. were contemplating taking legal action in the matter.

Acrimony and controversy surrounding what was known as the Lacca water scheme led to the election of 1928 being uncontested. Lacca was near Duagh and about seven kilometres south east of Listowel. A proposal to bring water from there to the town was placed before the council. It was pushed through against the wishes of a large majority of the members, who thereafter either were disqualified or resigned. This left Tom Walsh, Paddy Brown and E. J. Gleeson, who supported the scheme, to press ahead with it. The opposition to the scheme by members of the council and many of the townspeople was prompted by their conviction that the scheme would not be successful. There was also a suspicion about the motivation of several of the chief supporters of the scheme inside and outside the council. They had relatives with land in the area designated for the scheme.

In September 1929 a tender of £5,945 to complete the scheme was accepted from P. Henry, contractor. On 21 September 1931 the water from Lacca reached the town. In the event, the scheme did not provide the water-supply required. Subsequent attempts to supplement the scheme caused further problems. In a letter to the *Kerryman*[1] Dr Michael O'Connor of The Square noted that the 'Lacca scheme' had proved to be inadequate, as he had forecast, and was now to be supplemented from a stream near Toor Creamery, into which unsanitary effluent from the creamery was running.

Listowel Urban District Council, under the chairmanship of Jeremiah Buckley (Fianna Fáil) refused to strike a rate which would in effect pay for the failed water-scheme. They sought a meeting with the government who responded to their failure to strike a rate by dissolving the council and replacing it with a commissioner, John P. Moran of Limerick. A Citizen's Defence Committee was set up and obtained an injunction restraining Moran from striking a rate to pay for the water-scheme. The Committee was representative and the injunction was granted to Paddy Breen, William McElligott, Patrick Corridan, Jeremiah Buckley and the Reverend Robert Adderley.[2]

At first glance it would seem that the residue of bitterness from the civil war and the heightened factionalism which characterised the period was the main reason for the lack of a contest in the 1934 election. But, just as significantly, there was disillusionment with the running of the town council and few people were keen to attempt a resolution of the difficulties which arose from the failed water-scheme. This contributed also to the elections in 1942 and 1945 being uncontested.

1. *Kerryman* 22 September 1935.
2. For an account of how the failed water-scheme and the Citizen's Defence Committee caused deep and well-nigh disastrous divisions among members of the Listowel Race Committee, see J. O'Flaherty, *Listowel Races 1858-1992: a history,* pp.118-23.

By contrast from 1950 onwards there was an increasing interest in the elections to the town council. From 1960 the electorate steadily increased until it was 3,628 in 1999 and in the six elections beginning in 1967 an average of 70.28 per cent of the electorate voted. At this time also the council had the services of William Wixted and William Walsh. The former was town-clerk from 1969 to 1993 and the latter was the town engineer from 1977 to 1996.[3]

Development of the Town, Its Services and Amenities

The development of the town and its services and amenities since 1972 is a measure of the remarkable diligence of the councillors and their staff. The council provided public housing at Ballygologue Park (1972-79; 1993-96), at Feale Drive (1982-88), Courthouse Lawn (1992-4), Convent View (1998-2000), Dowd's Road (1996-) and John B. Keane Grove (1999-2001). In the 1970s and 1980s the council supervised the building of private houses at Ballygologue (Hawthorn Drive), Bridge Road (Woodlawn), Cahirdown (Aviation Drive, Gurtinard, Hollytree Drive, Woodview), Clieveragh (Clieveragh Park, Knockroe Drive, Luachra Road) and Dowd's Road (Cherrytree Drive).

In the 1990s through to 2003 private housing continued to be built at Ballygologue (Dromin Green, Meelish Close, The Forge), Bridge Road (The Lodge, The Paddocks), Cahirdown (Cluain Doire, College Lawn), Clieveragh (Clieveragh Downs, Lartigue Village, Slí na Spéire, Willow

---

3. Wixted was succeeded by Kieran O'Driscoll (1993), Joan McCarthy (1994-8), Karen Lynch (1998-2000), Kathleen Moriarty (2000-1), Gráinne O'Mahony (2001-2) and John Doody (2002 -). Walsh was succeeded by Paul Stack (1996-2002).

Brook), Dowd's Road (Willow Place) and Greenville (Ashfield, Ferndene).

To cope with the increase in traffic the council provided a new traffic route lighting system from 1973 onwards and introduced a one-way traffic system in 1980. It provided a car-park at the rear of Charles Street in 1981, widened roads and extended footpaths at Ballygologue Road, Clieveragh Road, Greenville Road, Library Road and Tralee Road in the 1980s. This was continued with the widening of the Ballybunion Road in the 1990s. The town's first traffic warden was appointed in 1994. There was a major upgrading of the Square and a re-routing of the N69 road around the former St John's Church in 1995-6. Further areas were designated as car-parks, at the rear of Upper William Street and the rear of the Castle in 1998-2000. A road named after John B. Keane and linking Upper Patrick Street and Ballygologue was laid along the disused railway line in 1998-2001. The footpaths in Church Street, Colbert Street, Main Street and William Street were re-furbished in 1999-2001. Finally on-street pay parking was introduced in 2000.

Apart from the Lacca Water Scheme fiasco, the provision of a satisfactory supply of clean water to the town posed serious problems over many years. This prompted the extension of the water treatment plant in the mid-1970s. Further improvement in the town's water-supply was ensured with the replacement of the watermains and the connection of the town to the North East Kerry Regional Water Supply in the early 1980s. In a major undertaking the main draining system was substantially upgraded in 1985-7 with the building of an effluent treatment plant at Gortnaminsha and the lining of the main culvert through the town.

The new emphasis at national level on the need to cherish the environment was reflected locally. The over-crowded cemetery was cleaned up and extended to an area at the rear of the Sportsfield in 1979. The town dump at Gurtinard was closed in 1988 and transmuted into the Garden of Europe in 1995. Wheeled refuse bins were introduced and a new cemetery was opened at the Ballybunion Road in 1994.

The councillors did not neglect the need for recreational facilities. At the Town Park they provided a pitch and putt course, tennis courts and playing pitches in the early 1970s, a Community Centre in 1985-6 and a children's playground in 1994. Heritage-conscious, they had the unique 'Dandy Lodge' relocated from Bridge Road to the Town Park in 1995-6, and the Millennium Arch erected at Bridge Road in 2000-1.

The promotion of commercial and industrial development was and continues to be a major concern for the town councillors. With their active support the Industrial Development Authority set up an industrial estate of thirty acres at Clieveragh between the late 1970s and early 1980s and five Enterprise Units in 1992.

Perhaps the most imaginative development during the past thirty years has been the establishment of the Civic Centre at the rear of Charles Street. Here the council sited 'Áras an Phiarsaigh', the new local authority offices, in 1989, the five Enterprise Units in 1992, the new library, after a design by Murray-Ó Laoire, in 1995 and a new fire station in 1997 with the court house which was substantially refurbished in the late 1990s. Here also is the Courthouse Lawn housing development.

Listowel Arms Hotel and St Patrick's Hall

Two major buildings were given a new lease of life, the Listowel Arms Hotel and St Patrick's Hall.

The group of Listowel business people, who bought the

hotel from Joseph McLoughlin (Locke) in 1963, added a new wing to it in 1970. They sold it to Tony Heaphy, from Duagh, in 1979. Heaphy re-sold it to the Murphy family, proprietors of the 'Dunraven Arms', Adare, in 1986. They were in possession until 1988, when it was bought by the Ryan family, proprietors of the 'Limerick Inn'.

The Ryans sold the hotel to the O'Callaghan family, from Moyvane, in 1996. In 1997 it was extensively refurbished and a large extension was completed in 2001. The Listowel Arms Hotel with the Cliff House Hotel in Ballybunion is now part of the O'Callaghan Family Group Hotels in North Kerry.

St Patrick's Hall continues as a general parish hall and is used by the community for a wide range of activities. At Writers' Week it is used as a centre for art exhibitions. It was substantially refurbished in 2002. The hall is administered by a management committee, the officers of which for 2003-4 were: Chairman: Canon James Linnane, Secretary: Ann Brassil and Treasurer: William Walsh.

There were closures. In 1966 the local branch of the National Bank, which had been established in the town in 1866 was closed. It was amalgamated with the adjacent branch of the Bank of Ireland, which had opened in 1870. Also in 1966 the local branch of the Provincial Bank, which was established in 1879, was re-named the Allied Irish Bank after the amalgamation of the Munster & Leinster Bank, Provincial Bank of Ireland and Royal Bank of Ireland. The railway station, unused for passengers since 1963 and for the carriage of goods since 1976, was formally closed in 1979.

The town councillors have been perceptive in their promotion of cultural and heritage projects and support for such events. Thus it was not surprising when the town was granted Heritage Status in 2000 and won first place in 2002 in the prestigious International Nations in Bloom

Competition (for towns with less than a population of 20,000). In accordance with the outward-looking trend in the 1980s and 1990s, the town was twinned with Downpatrick in 1983; Shawnee, Kansas, US, in 1986; Panissieres, France in 1992 and Los Gatos, California, US, in 1993.[4]

---

4. The above and Appendices 1 and 2 have been taken from D. Roche, *Local government in Ireland* (Dublin 1982), *passim*, J.J. Webb, *Municipal government in Ireland: medieval and modern* (Dublin 1918) p.267, *Listowel Urban District Council: local election results 1899-1999* (Listowel 1999), *passim* and information from William Walsh and William Wixted.

APPENDIX 1

Listowel Urban District/Town Councillors

1967-74

CHAIRMAN: Rotated on a yearly basis.[5] MEMBERS (in order of election):
Patrick (Patsy) Walsh (FF), Gerard Lynch (FG), Albert Kennedy (FF), Bernard Hanley (FG), Thomas Grogan (FF), Michael L. O'Connell (FG), Michael O'Neill (Ind.), J. D. Pierse (FG) and Thomas P. Walsh (FF)

1974-9

CHAIRMAN: Rotated. MEMBERS: Patsy Walsh (FF), Gerard Lynch (FG) Thomas P. Walsh (FF), Albert Kennedy (FF), J. D. Pierse (Ind.), Louis O'Connell (FG), Brendan Daly (FG), Michael O'Neill (Ind.) and Michael Barrett (FG)

1979-85

CHAIRMAN: Rotated. MEMBERS: Albert Kennedy (Ind.), Robert Pierse (FG), John Holly (SF), Gerard Lynch (FG), Maria Gorman (FF),[6] Michael Barrett (FG), Michael O'Neill (Ind.), Anthony (Tony) O'Callaghan (FF) and Thomas Walsh (FF)

---

5. There was an exception: Patsy Walsh served two consecutive terms as chairman in 1968-9 and 1969-70.
6. In May 1979, seemingly for electoral advantage, Maria O'Gorman submitted her name as Maria Gorman for the local elections. For the controversy surrounding this, see *Kerryman* 18 May 1979. She was not the first lady to serve in the Urban District Council. Mrs B. Foran was a member from 1908 to 1914 and Margaret (Maggie) Ashe served from 1920 to 1925. However, Maria O'Gorman was the first lady to chair the Council which she did in 1984-5.

1985-94

CHAIRMAN: Rotated. MEMBERS: Edward (Ned) O'Sullivan (FF), Donal Kelliher (SF), Michael Guerin (Lab.), Albert Kennedy (Ind.), Robert Pierse (FG), James Beasley (FG), Tony O'Callaghan (FF), Thomas P. Walsh (FF) and Denis Stack (FG)

1994-9

CHAIRMAN: Rotated. MEMBERS: Edward (Ned) O'Sullivan (FF), Mary Horgan (FG), Tony O'Callaghan (FF), Albert Kennedy (Ind.), Donal Kelliher (SF), Maria Gorman (FF), Louis O'Connell (FG), Denis Stack (FG) and Frank Pierse (FG)

1999-2004

CHAIRMAN/MAYOR: Rotated. MEMBERS: Ned O'Sullivan (FF), Timothy (Tim) O'Leary (FG), Jacqueline Barrett (FG), Denis Stack (FG), Louis O'Connell (FG), Maria Gorman (FF), Thomas (Tom) Walsh (FF), Anthony Curtin (SF) and Patrick (Pat) Loughnane[7]

---

7. Four families have been well represented in the Urban District Council during the past thirty-five years: Gerard Lynch (1967-79) and his daughter Mary Horgan (1994-9), Michael Louis O'Connell (1967-79) and his grandson Louis (1999-2004), John D. Pierse (1967-79) and his brothers Robert (1979-94) and Frank (1994-9) and Thomas P. Walsh (1967-94) and his son Thomas (1999-2004).

APPENDIX 2

The elected representatives for the Kerry North constituency embracing the Listowel area, 1973–2003

Twentieth Dáil: 1973
Lynch, Gerard, FG
McEllistrim, Thomas, FF
Spring, Daniel, Labour

Twenty-First Dáil: 1977
Ahern, Catherine (Kit), FF
McEllistrim, Thomas, FF
Spring, Daniel, Labour

Twenty-Second Dáil: 1981
Foley, Denis, FF
McEllistrim, Thomas, FF
Spring, Richard, Labour
(son of Daniel Spring above)

Twenty-Third Dáil: Feb. 1982
Same

Twenty Fourth Dáil: Nov. 1982
Same

Twenty-Fifth Dáil: 1987
Deenihan, James, FG
Foley, Denis, FF
Spring, Richard, Labour

Twenty-Sixth Dáil: 1989
Deenihan, James, FG
McEllistrim, Thomas, FF
Spring, Richard, Labour

Twenty-Seventh Dáil: 1992
Deenihan, James, FG
Foley, Denis, FF
Spring, Richard, Labour

Twenty-Eighth Dáil: 1997
Same

Twenty-Ninth Dáil: 2002
Deenihan, James, FG
Ferris, Martin, SF
McEllistrim, Thomas FF
(son of Thomas
McEllistrim above)

APPENDIX 3

CIVIC ORGANISATIONS[8]

Listowel Business & Retailers Association

This organisation had its roots in a committee of Listowel traders which was set up in 1894 to prepare a harvest festival in connection with the annual autumn race-meeting. Subsequently it was involved with other festival committees to this end.

Then in the early 1970s it was formally established as the Listowel Traders Association. Its remit was limited to: (1) organising Christmas retail promotions, including town lighting, sales promotions, newspaper advertising features and radio campaigns and (2) representing the business community at Listowel Urban District Council and Kerry County Council on issues such as the striking of the rates, parking charges and town development. In 1997 it had 120 members and changed its name to the Listowel Business & Retailers Association and was registered as such in 1999.

In May 2000, representatives of the Association attended a preliminary meeting with a view to establishing a Chamber of Commerce in Listowel. The Association set up a steering committee, on which its members were represented, to this end. It met in January 2001. In October of the same year this steering committee made a formal application to the Chamber of Commerce of Ireland for associate membership. In the application it was stated that the

8. Information on these provided by officers of the organisations listed.

Listowel Business & Retailers Association intended to amalgamate its organisation into the Chamber of Commerce of Ireland structure.

There has been no urgency since then in this regard. The Association's officers in 2003-4 were: Chairman: Charles Cantillon, Secretary: Mary Horgan and Treasurer: Oonagh Harnett.

Listowel Chamber of Commerce

In May 2000, on the initiative of Deputy Jimmy Deenihan and representatives of Listowel Business & Retailers Association, a meeting was held to establish a Chamber of Commerce in the town. On 13 June 2002, after careful preparation, the Chamber was formally launched. It adopted as its mission statement:

> The mission of Listowel Chamber of Commerce is to serve and represent the interests of the business community of Listowel and its environs and to stimulate and promote the economic development of the area in partnership with other organisations. In doing so the Chamber aims to provide a value for money, trade and business information service to the business community of the Listowel area.

The Listowel Business & Retailers Association and its antecedent organisation had represented the commercial interests of the town during the previous thirty years and had 120 members. It was hoped that the new organisation would, in effect, be an enlargement of the Retailers Association so as to include the interests of the tourism and professional services sectors.

At the first annual general meeting of the Chamber of

Commerce on 20 November 2003 it was reported that the committee had lobbied, albeit not with much success, for a better direct road link between the town and the National Primary Road Network, that Listowel's Chamber of Commerce had been affiliated to the Chambers of Commerce of Ireland and that the 'Tourism sub-group' with the help of Shannon Development had produced a brochure 'Destination Listowel/Destination Ballybunion'.

The committee for 2003-4 was: President: Heinrich Weber; Members: John Galvin, Hugh Joyce, Simon McKenna, John O'Sullivan, Mark Prendiville, Derry Reen, Kay Sayers and Cara Trant.

Listowel Credit Union

From the 1970s onwards the Irish Credit Union Movement showed what could be achieved by local communities when they exercised initiative and had confidence in themselves. A branch was established in Listowel on 7 March 1973 and the following officers were appointed: Chairman: Michael Moore, Secretary: Maria O'Gorman, Treasurer: Timothy O'Flaherty.

The office of the branch was located in the former Listowel Technical School (1973-4), 13 Ashe Street (1974-80), 69 Charles Street (1980-5) and 69 Ashe Street (1985-2001). In 2001 the branch moved into its splendid new premises on the site of the former Rendezvous Bar and Listowel Auto Services.

The annual financial statement for the year ending in September 2003 reported savings of €41 million and loans of €19 million. In 2003-4 the branch had a staff of seven, one of whom was part time, and 14,000 members. The officers were: Chairman: Christopher Killeen, Secretary: Kim Heffernan, Treasurer: Leo Daly and Manager: Denis Dillane.

Listowel Food Fair

This food fair, now the second largest in the country, has been held each November since 1995. It was initiated by Deputy Jimmy Deenihan, when he was junior minister for agriculture. The aim of the fair is to increase awareness and appreciation of the range and quality of Irish food products through seminars, workshops, cookery demonstrations, tastings and competitions.

Each year the food fair has a main theme. In 2003 the fair hosted the first National Farmhouse Cheese Competition. Thirty-seven cheeses were entered from twenty-four cheese makers from around the country.

The committee, which organises the fair, is chaired by Deputy Deenihan and its secretary is Johanna Watkins.

The Rotary Club of Listowel

The Rotary Club of Listowel was set up by Maurice O'Sullivan on 14 June 1986 to promote community projects. In 1994 it helped to provide an Adventure Playground for children in the Town Park. In the following year it was instrumental in establishing the Garden of Europe in Gurtinard. This garden of over 3,000 trees and shrubs was located on the site of the former Town Dump. At one end there is a monument to the profundity and diversity of European civilisation in the guise of a bust of Schiller, author of the European anthem, *Ode to Joy*, which was set to the music of Beethoven's Ninth Symphony. At the other end is a memorial to those who died in the Holocaust, and to all victims of injustice and oppression.

The officers of the Club in 2003-4 were: President: Patrick Fitzgibbon; Secretary: Paul O'Dowd and Treasurer: Gerard Leahy.

COMMERCIAL AND INDUSTRIAL DEVELOPMENT

During the past thirty years one of the remarkable features of Listowel has been its commercial and industrial development. As elsewhere in the country, there was high unemployment and emigration in this area in the 1940s and 1950s. Then the *Programme for Economic Expansion* was published at the end of 1958. This proposed a shift from protection to free trade, from discouragement to encouragement of foreign investment and the directing of public expenditure from social to productive investment.

The challenge in the programme to seek out foreign investment was taken up in many places by local public representatives, not least Daniel J. Moloney, Fianna Fáil TD for North Kerry from 1957 to 1961. A native of Lyracrompane, he was a garage proprietor in Listowel. Early in 1960 he and other Listowel business people formed the Listowel Industrial Development Association. A few months later the group published and distributed a brochure *Facilities for industrialists – what Listowel has to offer*.

Imperial Stag Ltd

Before the Association had been formally established some

of its members, including Deputy Moloney, had been in contact with the Weber family of Solingen in West Germany. Because of increasing labour costs in their own country, they were at that time on the point of transferring their factory elsewhere. After brief negotiations with a representative delegation from the town the Weber family moved their knife production operation to Listowel in 1960. The company was named Jowika (Ireland) Ltd and was in full production in 1961. It was initially managed by Eugene Weber and his son Heinrich and produced pocket (folding) knives and some fixed blade hunting knives. They also sold table knives which were bought in from other manufacturers.

In 1974 the company was purchased by a company in the US and traded under the name of Cole National Inc. In 1977 Cole National Inc. sold the company to the Imperial Schrade Corporation. It was re-named Stag Cutlery Ltd. Throughout the buy-outs Heinrich Weber remained as director and general manager of the plant. In 1986 the company became Imperial Stag Ltd.

From the outset the factory employed about a hundred people. This rose to 120, as well as ten to fifteen outdoor and part-time workers. These last were housewives who were paid on a piece-work basis. Employer-employee relations were excellent. Some employees were collected by minibus from outlying areas and at one time the company had twenty people with forty years service.

With the enlargement of the plant and modern machinery, production rose to two million units per year and a turnover in excess of €5 million. About 65 per cent of the knives were sold in the US and the rest in almost every country in the world. In 2001 Henry Weber retired from the company. By 2003 the company was still in production but, like most other manufacturers, was seriously affected by the world economic recession.[1]

Kerry Group plc

The most notable economic event in Listowel and, indeed, the whole county, during the past thirty years, has been the development of North Kerry Milk Products Limited, the forerunner of Kerry Co-op and Kerry Group, into a global ingredients, flavours and consumer foods business. This began with the milk processing plant which was established in the 'Canon's field' on the Tralee Road in 1972. It manufactured a milk protein product called Casein, an ingredient with many applications in the food and beverages industry. This was exported to the American Erie Casein Company of Illinois. The American company held a 15 per cent share of the original North Kerry company and the remaining shares were held by the Dairy Disposal Company, on the one hand, and eight local co-operative creameries, on the other. The plant had a daily intake of 150,000 gallons of milk and employed 50 people. In 1973 a subsidiary plant for producing skimmed milk powder for export was established beside the main factory. This plant also had an intake of 150,000 gallons of milk and employed another 50 people. The following year a whey-processing plant was opened on the site.

In 1973 Ireland joined the European Economic Community (EEC) and this accelerated the merger of many small dairies in Ireland so as to be able to compete with the larger milk companies in the existing EEC. Kerry Co-op followed suit and with an injection of capital from milk

1. *Facilities for industrialists – what Listowel has to offer* (Listowel 1960) and information from Oliver O'Neill, administration manager, Imperial Stag Ltd, 1980-2000.

suppliers in the county it acquired the State-owned milk processing company and its creameries, together with its 42.5 per cent stake in the private NKMP company for a consideration of €1.5 million. Furthermore, six of the eight independent co-ops, which held the other 42.5 per cent, were acquired and accordingly the private company became a subsidiary of the newly formed Kerry Co-operative Creameries Ltd (Kerry Co-op) which began trading in January 1974.

Next the company set about acquiring regional dairies: Killarney in 1975, Limerick in 1978, Ballinahina (Cork) in 1979, Deel (Rathkeale) in 1979, Galway in 1982, Moate in 1986 and Tuam in 1992. These were re-organised into one integrated unit selling a wide range of milk and butter products, as well as low-fat spreads – all under the Dawn brand.

The 1980s saw the company diversify by expanding into the pork meat business. In 1982 Henry Denny & Sons Ltd at Tralee was acquired, as was Duffy Meats Ltd of Hacketstown. The former had a wide range of products which included ham, bacon and sausage, the latter sold an array of cooked meats, many for export. This segment of Kerry Group's business was rounded off with the acquisition of Denny's factory in Portadown in 1988 and the opening of a processing plant at Shillelagh in 1994, a facility which today employs more than 700 people.

With food ingredients becoming central to food production the Kerry management planned to expand into that branch of the food business in the US. To this end, in 1984 they bought out the interest held by the Erie Casein Company of Illinois in North Kerry Milk Products. This was the company which had enabled them to gain a toehold in the US market. In 1986, with the approval of Kerry farmers who were the shareholders of Kerry Co-operative

Creameries (Kerry Co-op), a public company was launched. Essentially it involved the formation of a Public Limited Company (Kerry Group plc) by acquiring the undertaking, property and assets of the Co-op and as a consideration 90 million ordinary shares in Kerry Group plc were issued to the Co-op. Then in October 1986 a public offering of shares in Kerry Group plc was made at 66 cent (IR52 pence) per share and the shares were listed on the Dublin stock exchange.

Subsequent to the successful launch and establishment of Kerry Group plc in 1986, higher growth targets were agreed which, with the requisite capital available, were achieved predominantly by acquisitions at home and overseas. In 1988 the Kerry company acquired Beatreme Food Ingredients. Based in Beloit, Wisconsin, it was the leading such firm with a significant market share in the US food ingredients business and was acquired by Kerry for US$130m. The acquisition of Beatreme in 1988 opened markets for Kerry throughout the world and provided a platform for Kerry's growth and development into a leading global food ingredients corporation. This acquisition was a watershed, marking Kerry Group's transformation from a regional to an international food business.

In the meantime, the company became involved in a number of beef businesses at home. When the profit margin in these remained too slim, due to EU market issues, the Group quickly re-sold them. The company had more success in other areas. In 1988 Kerry Group became a major player in the poultry market after acquiring Grove Farm/Ballyfree. And in 1990 it entered the duck and goose and the lamb market in the UK, buying A.E. Button and Sykes Ltd and North Yorkshire Lamb Co respectively.

On the international scene the acquisition of Beatreme Food Ingredients was but an earnest of what was to come.

Kerry Group plc absorbed into its overall structure Milac GmbH of Wadersloh, Germany, in 1990; Dairyland of Minnesota, US; Eastleigh Flavours, UK, and W.L. Miller & Robirch, UK in 1991; Northland Foods, Owen, Wisconsin, in 1992; Malcolm Foods, St George, Ontario, Research Foods, Toronto, and Tingles Ltd, Portsmouth, in 1993; DCA Food Industries Inc., in the US, Mattessons & Walls and Margetts Foods, UK, and Productos Vegetales de Mexico at Irapuato, in 1994.

By 1994 all of Kerry's consumer foods operations in Ireland and the UK had been combined under the Kerry Foods structure of six business units. After acquiring Kerry Spring Mineral Water, located in Ballyferriter, Co. Kerry, the company was challenging Ballygowan for premier place in that market. The pork product business was based in Dublin. The dairies unit was centred in Tralee. Specialty poultry products were based in Norfolk in the UK. The foods division was now directed from Egham, outside London. North American operations were directed from Beloit, Wisconsin, US.

Kerry's drive to be a significant player in the global food business gathered momentum from 1996 onwards. The company acquired Ciprial S.A., Lyons & Apt, France, DCA, Solutech, Australia in 1996; SDF Foods, Malaysia, and G.R. Spinks, UK, in 1997; Burns-Philip & Co. Ltd, Australia and New Zealand, Dalgety Food Ingredients, US, Star & Arty Ingredientes Alimenticios, LTDA, Sao Paulo, Brazil and a manufacturing plant at Tres Coracoes, Minas Gerais, Brazil, in 1998; Shade Foods Inc., US, and Tukania Proca GmbH, Rodgau, Germany, in 1999; and Armour Food Ingredients, US, in 2000. The Golden Vale businesses, predominantly located in Ireland and the UK, were acquired and successfully integrated in 2001. 2002 and 2003 saw the further acquisition of well known food businesses in Brazil, Canada, France,

Ireland, Italy, Mexico, Thailand, UK and US.

In his comprehensive account of Kerry Group plc, James P. Kennelly justifiably attributed most credit for the success of the company to a triumvirate of Eddie Hayes, Frank Wall and Denis Brosnan. Eddie Hayes, a farmer from Kilflynn, led a campaign for many years for a milk-processing factory to serve the farmers and people of North Kerry. Frank Wall, a farmer from Tarbert and as influential as Hayes in farming circles, played a vital role in ensuring that the farmers of Kerry united into Kerry Co-operative Creameries Ltd (Kerry Co-op), the bedrock of Kerry Group plc.

Denis Brosnan was born in Kilflynn on 29 November 1944. Educated at the local national school, St Brendan's seminary, Killarney, and University College, Cork, his first work experience was selling industrial detergents in Ireland for a Scottish company. After less than a year he joined the staff of Golden Vale Creameries Ltd for whom he was a foreign sales manager in London in 1970 and 1971. He was appointed general manager of North Kerry Milk Products Ltd in December 1971 and became managing director and chairman of the board of Kerry Group plc in February 1986. For over thirty years he led the Kerry enterprise to undreamt of success in the ruthlessly competitive world of the international foods business.

While much of the credit for the success of Kerry Group has been given to Brosnan, he was ably assisted by gifted colleagues, not least Hugh Friel and Denis Cregan, the Group's deputy managing directors. On 1 January 2002 Brosnan stepped down from the top post in Kerry Group and was succeeded by Hugh Friel as managing director and on 1 August 2003 he retired as chairman of the board and director of the Group to be replaced by Denis Buckley, who hails from Tullamore, Listowel. In 2003 the other executive directors of the company were Michael Griffin, Stan

McCarthy and Brian Mehigan. They presided over a company which had 20,000 employees and 150 manufacturing facilities across 17 countries in all five continents with an annual turnover of €4 billion. The company is quoted on the Dublin and London stock exchanges with a share value of €2.8 billion and some 30,000 shareholders.

Notwithstanding its transformation into a global food business Kerry Group plc retained its strong links with Kerry in general and Listowel in particular. The head office with a staff of 140 continued to be sited in Tralee. In 2003, approximately 50 per cent of the company's shares were held by residents of Kerry, including a 31 per cent share-holding by Kerry Co-op, i.e. the farmers of Kerry. Of the company's Irish workforce of 5,000, 1,000 were employed in Kerry, making it the largest industrial employer in the county. In addition, some 3,000 Kerry milk suppliers were dependent on the income derived from the milk they supplied to the company. And in 2003, 500 were employed at the factory in Listowel where it all began in 1972.[2]

Listal Ltd

Listal Ltd is an Irish company which manufactures medical filters for the world's healthcare markets. It was established in 1993 by a group of British, Irish and Italian businessmen which included the present board of directors: M. Boiero, P. Casey, G. Guala and D. Irvine. Ireland was chosen as the site for the company's market when it became clear that the current managing director, Patrick (Pat) Casey, was available

---

2. James P. Kennelly, *The Kerry Way: The History of Kerry Group 1972-2000* (Dublin 2001) *passim* and information from Frank Hayes, director of corporate affairs, Kerry Group plc.

to head up the local manufacturing site. He had had many years of experience in the design and manufacture of medical filters as he had initiated and managed an American company producing similar products in Newcastle West. The company sited its operation in Listowel, owing to the ready availability of a 20,000 sq. feet factory. Another deciding factor was its close proximity to Casey's home.

Contrary to popular belief the company name was not derived from Listowel. The name is derived from two sources. The 'Lis' is from the name Lister who was the developer of antiseptic and the 'tal' is a reference to the sister company in Italy.

Initially Listal manufactured filters for supply to its Italian partner company only. However, as the company prospered it developed new products which are now sold worldwide. To stay abreast of the ever-increasing demand and to ensure a competitive sales price it has a policy of investing in state of the art machines with particular emphasis on automation.

Listal's compliance with international standards is a guarantee of high quality products for customers. These are used in blood transfusion sets, intravenous sets (drip units), hypodermic syringes and kidney dialysis machines. To supply a worldwide demand, Listal manufactures hundreds of millions of medical filters each year.

The process of making medical filters mainly involves injection moulding where the filter media is inserted in the hardened steel mould and molten plastic is injected around this media effectively making a plastic frame which will hold a very precise filter material in place. The process is carried out in a controlled working environment referred to as a cleanroom. This entails taking the outside air, cleaning and filtering it to a very high standard before circulating it into the working area. All parts when manufactured are visually inspected and then go to quality control for final inspection.

The factory operates six days a week, twenty-four hours a day. Its well-trained and highly motivated workforce of 70 is drawn from Listowel and its vicinity.[3]

Melchert Electronics Ltd

This factory was established in the Clieveragh Industrial Estate, Listowel, in 1977.

Lothar Melchert, owner and managing director, had earlier set up Melchert Elektronik GmbH, his printed circuit board business, in Cologne, West Germany. The demands of the industry at the time required two styles of technology, the simpler single sided 'punch and crunch' printed circuit board (pcb) and the more complex double sided through hold plated board. Each required different production lines. Following an offer by the Industrial Development Authority (IDA) of an attractive package of tax-breaks, advance factory facilities, proximity to Shannon Airport and an educated workforce Herr Melchert opened his factory in Listowel.

Herr Hartmut Reupert trained the workforce and in the early months ensured that orders came from the parent-business in Cologne. The plant prospered and at one period had 150 employees. It sold its pcbs to multinational companies such as IBM, Nixdorf, Timex, Siemens, Kostal and Nokia, as well as developing a home market. An ongoing policy of reinvestment and improvement saw an effluent plant, new plating hall and gold etchant line with laboratory support installed.

In 1987 Krupp Atlas, the ship building manufacturer, bought Melchert Elektronik GmbH in Cologne. The Listowel factory was included in the sale. It soon became

---

3. Information from Patrick Casey, managing director, Listal Ltd.

clear that for Krupp Atlas the Listowel factory was 'surplus to requirements'. With the support of Shannon Development this led to a management buyout of the plant which was re-named Munster Electronics (Mel).

The new company held its own market share and continued to develop its base with lucrative specialised contracts in Scandinavia where it supplied Ericsson, Danfoss and other well-known companies. However, eventually, it was not able to compete with factories in the Far East with regard to prices and quick response to customers' needs. After protracted Union negotiations Mel ceased to operate in 1997.

For a short time a new company came on site: Celtic Circuits making pcbs. It continued for three years. Notwithstanding the skills of its 33-strong workforce, many of whom had been trained by the original Melchert team, it also succumbed to the dictates of the market-place.[4]

Neodata Services Ltd

The company which became Neodata Services Inc. was established in Boulder, Colorado, USA in 1949. It set up a centre in Limerick in 1969. Because of the success of the centre in Limerick other centres were established in Abbeyfeale, Dingle, Kilmallock, Listowel and Newcastle West. The work done by Neodata Services in Ireland was the processing of orders for magazine subscriptions. Apart from those in Abbeyfeale and Dingle, each of the Irish centres flourished for almost twenty-five years.

The centre in Listowel began operations in 1971 and was employing 95 typists by 1973. Clients included Condé Nast which published *Vanity Fair*, *GQ*, *Vogue*, etc. The

4. Information from Elizabeth O'Reilly, an employee from 1982 to 2000.

centre also processed orders for a variety of children's magazines such as *Sesame Street* and *3+2+1 Contact*.

Throughout the 1970s and 1980s Neodata Services Ltd in Ireland was a very successful business. However, at the end of 1993 the global operations of Neodata Services Inc. were re-structured and this involved transferring its magazine subscription processing back to the US. This led to the closure in 1994 of the remaining Irish centres, apart from the one at Listowel.

The management and staff of 102 at Listowel were determined to ensure that their centre continued as an independent, viable enterprise. Alternative contracts were successfully negotiated, including lucrative ones with the Philip Morris Company to process its cigarette promotions. Such was the determination of the staff and management to see that their centre survived that when deadlines for completing contracts approached the staff would rise to almost 300 and the office would remain open to facilitate work on a 24-hour basis.

By the beginning of 1997, owing to developments in technology, the Philip Morris Company requested that some of the equipment at the Listowel centre be replaced at considerable cost. When it became clear that grant aid to this end was not available, the Listowel centre closed on 4 April 1997.[5]

Radlink Ltd

This company was a subsidiary of Schmittenberg and Ganseuer of Wuppertal, Germany, and was originally known

---

5. Information from the Irish Development Authority and Noreen McAuliffe, supervisor at Neodata Services Ltd, Listowel, 1977-1997.

as Schmiga Metal Works Ltd. It was established in Listowel in 1969 to manufacture steel components for the central heating radiator market in Britain. Before the company began production in 1970 its owner, Heinz Otto Schmittenberg was killed at a car rally in October 1969. The company was changed to UK ownership. Its name was changed to Stelrad Components and Peter Adams was appointed manager.

From the outset the company employed 20 people. Employment increased steadily through the 1970s and 1980s and reached a peak at 84, when the factory operated three shifts and was producing about 15 million components a year. In the early 1990s cost competition increased externally and from within the Group. This led in 1993 to 18 voluntary redundancies. In 1995 the Group indicated its intention to move the operation to one of their other factories in the UK. When the local management resisted this they were given an opportunity to buy-out the company, which they did. The company was re-named Radlink Ltd. However, owing to a lack of support on the part of some employees, the new enterprise was not successful. This led to the management closing the operation in May 1999 before the company became insolvent.[6]

Spectra Photo

Ireland's leading photo-processing company was established by Xavier McAuliffe in Listowel in 1970. He was born in the town on 7 June 1945 and was educated at the local national school and vocational school.

After spending four years as a freelance photographer, he

6. Information from Peter Adams, manager, 1970-1999.

recognised the acute need for an efficient photo-processing service. To this end he set up a laboratory at 27 Church Street in 1968 and began to supply a number of chemist shops in North Kerry. With due attention to customer needs and after sale service, the business grew. This growth was remarkable after the company introduced a mail-order service in 1976 and initiated a twenty-four hour service to customers in the early 1980s. In 1983 the company joined with An Post to initiate a new postal delivery service called Post Photo, whereby films could be processed and paid for by using any post office nationwide.

Such was the success of the company that it was able in 1994 to purchase Dublin-based Foto King, its biggest rival in the Republic of Ireland. Four years later it took over Belfast-based Belmont Foto, another major photo-processing company. Also in 1998 it acquired the Irish branch of Kodak Consumer Imaging. This led to the establishment of Speko, a distribution company for Kodak products in Ireland. In 2001 Spectra took over Cork-based Trucolor, adding a further 400 dealers. With its attention to research and development the company kept up with technological developments which revolutionised the photographic industry.

In 1979 Spectra transferred its head office and Listowel laboratory to the Clieveragh industrial estate where the head office of Speko was also sited in 1999.

In 2003 Spectra Photo had three main laboratories in Listowel, Dublin and Belfast and mini-laboratories in Dublin, Limerick, Waterford and Cork. Its outlets included 40 retail shops and over 1,500 dealers nationwide, it accounted for over 50 per cent of the photo-processing market and was developing five million films annually for customers which included those of Boots, the chain of chemist shops..

In 1985 Xavier McAuliffe and his colleagues on the board of Spectra Photo launched into the hotel business. By 2003 Spectra Group Hotels owned and operated Aguia Negra, Vilanculos, Mozambique; Barrow Country House, Tralee; Erinvale Estate Hotel, Cape Town, South Africa; Hans Merensky Golf and Country Club, Kruger National Park, Phalaborwa, South Africa; Kilkenny River Court Hotel; Van Rieebeck Hotel, Cape Town, South Africa, as well as the Helicopter Charter Service, Kerry International Airport, Killarney.

The company had also invested in the security business in the guise of Sentry Security and in housing developments in Ireland and the UK.

In 2003 Spectra Group: the photographic industry and the hotel and other business projects employed 600 with an annual turn-over of €50 million and budget of €1.5 million for advertising and promotions.[7]

---

7. Information from Xavier McAuliffe. See also *Sunday Tribune* 29 June 2003.

EDUCATION

Scoileanna Réalta na Maidne

Scoileanna Réalta na Maidne continued from 1973 onwards to be two schools, a junior school and a senior school, each with its own principal and staff, until they were amalgamated in 1984. During the past thirty years the new child-centred curriculum, introduced in 1971, has remained basically the same, except for a partial revision in 1999. In 1975, as elsewhere, the management of the school was transferred from the parish priest to a board of management, which consisted of the parish priest, or someone nominated by him, as chairman, with two representatives of the teaching staff, two representatives of the parents and three members nominated by the bishop. In 2000 the department of education extended the personnel of the board to include two extra members chosen by the original board members from the parish community and at the same time reduced the members nominated by the bishop from 3 to 2. At that time also the department required each board to facilitate the establishment of parents' associations.

For the school year 2003-4 Scoil Réalta na Maidne had a staff of 9, including the principal, John McAuliffe, and 168 pupils.[1]

Gael-Scoil, Lios Tuathail

Following representations from parents, who were eager to have their children in a school where Irish was the language of instruction and communication among teachers, children and management, the Gael-Scoil was established in September 1993. It began in the home of the O'Sullivan family at Ballygologue Cross with one teacher and seven pupils. Also on these premises was a Naíonra teacher with seven other pupils.

The following autumn the school, with two teachers and 20 pupils, transferred to a former mini-market nearby. Before the Christmas break it received Aitheantas (official recognition) from the Department of Education which thereafter supplied the school with pre-fab classrooms. Two years later the school had 49 pupils. It continued to flourish and by 2002 it had five teachers, including a resource teacher, and 86 pupils. Máire S. Uí Chonchúir was cathaoirleach of the board of management from 1993 to 2000 and was succeeded by Tadhg Ó Laoire who served from 2000 to 2003.[2]

---

1. Information from John McAuliffe and Sister Eileen Randles.
2. Information from Máire S. Uí Chonchúir. See also Máire S. Uí Chonchúir, 'A Dream Comes True – Gael-Scoil, Lios Tuathail,' *Shannonside Journal* (1996) pp.5-6

SECONDARY

Community College, Listowel

The Community College, Listowel is under the management of the Vocational Education Committee of the Kerry Education Service, which celebrated a hundred years of public education in Kerry in 2003. The first teacher appointed to the Listowel school under the system, known then as the Kerry County Agricultural and Technical Instruction Programme, was Michael Reidy from Tralee. He took up his appointment in September 1903. An accomplished craftsman and artist, examples of his work can be seen on the façade of Galvin's of William Street, the entrance to the Dick Fitzgerald Stadium in Killarney and the illustrations in the earlier books of 'An Seabhach'.

The first school was conducted in a premises in Market Street. This was replaced by a purpose-built Technical School at the mid-town end of Church Street in 1928. The present building at College Road was completed in 1966. An extension, which included a canteen, assembly area, science, language and social studies rooms, was added in 1990.

Under the Vocational Education Act 1930, the first Education Act passed by a native Irish government, the Group Certificate Examination was introduced in 1940. This gave access to apprenticeships in semi-state bodies and private industry. Together with the Intermediate Certificate Examination, it was replaced by the Junior Certificate Examination in 1989.

In the late 1960s, in addition to technical instruction and preparing pupils for the Group Certificate, the staff of the Vocational School had initiated courses for the Intermediate and Leaving Certificate examinations. Pupils from the school first sat the Intermediate examination in 1969 and the Leaving Certificate in 1971. Between 1972 and 1976, there was a sharing of facilities between St Michael's and the Vocational School. This was promoted and organised by An tAthair Diarmuid Ó Súilleabháin, president of St Michael's, Michael Gaine, vice principal, and Patrick Drummond, principal of the Vocational School. It involved pupils from St Michael's attending classes in agricultural science and agricultural economics in the Vocational School, and pupils from the Vocational School attending classes in mathematics in St Michael's.

From 1977 to 1990 there were special pre-employment courses. These were designed to prepare pupils for specific areas of employment and included work experience modules. The Technical School, which had become the Vocational School under the 1930 Act, was renamed the Community College, Listowel, in 1990, not least because of the wide range of services it provided.

Between 1976 and 2003 the number of day pupils gradually declined from 380 (258 boys and 122 girls) to 166 (156 boys and 10 girls). By contrast, in 2003 enrolments for adult education night classes were 662 (157 males and 505 females). From 1951 onwards, the school had facilitated University College, Cork, in providing the Social Science Diploma Course, inspired by Alfred O'Rahilly, president of UCC. Further night classes were inaugurated in 1977 and by the early 1980s over 360 were attending them. From the mid-1990s onwards the College responded to the need and demand for training in computers, classes in commerce and courses in childcare, within the post Leaving-Certificate sector. In 1998-9 there were 44 day students enrolled in courses under the Vocational Training Opportunities Scheme (VTOS). The scheme was aimed mainly at adults who had left school without any qualification and were on social welfare. In 2002 the Back to Education Initiative programme was introduced leading to qualifications on a whole range of subjects under the Further Education and Training Awards Council (FETAC).

In 2003 the College had a full-time teaching staff of ten as well as 20 part-time teachers. Two of the principals have been long-serving: Patrick Drummond, 1955-76 and Patrick O'Sullivan, 1976-97. Thomas Fitzgerald served as principal from 1997 to 2002, when he was succeeded by Seán McCarthy, a former president of the Teachers' Union of Ireland. Michael Gaine, vice-principal since 1970, has been acting-principal on several occasions during the past 34 years.[3]

St Michael's College

An tAthair Diarmuid Ó Súilleabháin who was appointed president of St Michael's in 1972 was determined to extend the range of subjects in the College. He added French and musicianship to the curriculum. He also enabled pupils to take classes in agricultural economics and agricultural science in the nearby Vocational School. The addition of these new subjects to the curriculum marked the ending of the College's proud classical tradition. Greek was phased out in 1972, Latin in 1975.

By that time the policy of the Department of Education was to rationalise educational facilities, wherever possible. An tAthair Ó Súilleabháin was personally persuaded of the need to centralise second-level education in the town. For a number of years much discussion and serious consideration was given to, at first, a proposal to amalgamate Listowel

---

3. Information from Michael Gaine, Seán McCarthy and Patrick (Patsy) O'Sullivan.

Vocational School, St Michael's College and the Presentation Secondary School, and later, to the amalgamation of the Vocational School and St Michael's. That neither of these proposals were acted on was due not least to the stiff opposition of most of the staff at St Michael's and many of the townspeople who were determined that the much-valued distinctive tradition of the College would be preserved.

No sooner had Fr Patrick J. Horgan succeeded An tAthair Ó Súilleabháin in 1978 than he was involved in preparations for the celebration of the College's centenary. In early June 1979 there was a thanksgiving Mass in St Mary's, at which Mgr Patrick Quille, a past pupil and administrator of Edinburgh' cathedral, was the homilist, and a centenary banquet at the Devon Inn Hotel, Templeglantine. *St Michael's College, Listowel 1879-1979*, a splendid compilation of articles by presidents, teachers and *alumni*, was published as a centenary souvenir. Soon afterwards Fr Horgan unveiled ambitious plans for a major extension of the College and to this end a fund-raising committee was set up.

Eventually the large-scale extension to the College was formally opened by Donal Creed, junior minister of education, in September 1985. A Mass to mark the occasion was celebrated by Bishop Ó Súilleabháin, the former president of the College, and the homilist was Fr J. Anthony Gaughan, a former pupil. The new extension involved nine classrooms, a staff room, offices for the principal and secretary and a large sports hall. There were also a computer room, a demonstration room for 60 pupils, modern language room, science facilities, library and assembly area. In addition, the project included the installation of central heating, new windows and furniture in the original building. The substantial increase in the College premises was timely as by then it had a staff of 20 and 325 pupils.

A 'Millennium Ball' (dinner-dance) was held in the Listowel Arms Hotel on 17 December 1999 to mark the 120th anniversary of the founding of the College. In his message to the staff and pupils Bishop William (Bill) Murphy noted: 'On one of the pillars which one passes when entering St Michael's College is its motto – *Quis ut Deus* – which can be translated "God first".' He continued: 'Past generations recognised God in their lives and, indeed, many become priests and devoted themselves to spreading the Christian message at home and throughout the world.' And he concluded: 'In the College's 120 years of existence thousands of boys from North Kerry and West Limerick have been grateful for the opportunities which have been given by the dedicated service of the staff of St Michael's.'

A further extension to St Michael's was formally opened by An Taoiseach, Bertie Ahern, TD, and blessed by Fr Patrick Crean-Lynch in September 2003. The College's facilities were thereby enhanced with a wood-technology room, a metal-technology room, art and science rooms, as well as changing-rooms and showers for those involved in physical education sessions. The occasion was also marked by the official opening of the College's newly stocked library.

For the academic year 2003-4 the College had 22 teachers and 221 pupils.[4]

---

4. *St Michael's College, Listowel 1879-1979* (Listowel 1979) p.127; Booklet (St Michael's College, Millennium Ball 17 December 1999); *Kerryman* 25 May, 8 June 1979; 20 September 1985; 25 September 2003 and information from Canon Patrick J. Horgan, John Molyneux and John Mulvihill. For the presidents and teachers of St Michael's College: 1973-2003, see Appendix 1.

SCHOOLS AND COMMUNITY SERVICES OF THE PRESENTATION SISTERS

From 1973 onwards the Presentation Sisters continued in their role as educators of girls in Listowel and its hinterland in their primary and secondary schools. In October 1985 they opened an extension to their secondary school. The new extended school, Meán Scoil Mhuire Fatima, had 31 teachers and 485 pupils. It was equipped to provide the new programmes which the Department of Education was bringing on stream. These were intended to cater for the needs of all students. Thus fifth year students were given the option of following any of the department's Leaving Certificate programmes – Leaving Certificate Applied, Leaving Certificate Vocational Programme or transition year – from the 1990s onwards.

In September 1990 a new primary school was erected on a site on the Ballybunion Road donated by the sisters. It replaced the original primary school built in 1883. The new school had 11 teachers and 360 pupils. On the same site the sisters built the Nano Nagle school for mentally and physically handicapped children. This had 12 teachers and 60 pupils. The unique placing of the two schools on the same campus ensured their interaction and was applauded by educationalists and non-educationalists alike.

After the Second Vatican Council religious congregations and orders, including the Presentation Sisters, embarked on a programme of renewal. Essential to this was a determination to return to the spirit, as well as the letter, of their founding intention. This led the Presentation Sisters to re-focus their mission more directly on the marginalised and the poor. In so doing they were also adapting to radical changes in Ireland, where remarkable progress had been made to ensure that all children had access to both primary and secondary education.

From the 1970s onwards the effect of this renewal on the Presentation Sisters in Listowel was evident in a number of ways. Earlier, after widespread consultation, the Presentation Sisters in Ireland had amalgamated into a Union, forming three provinces. South West province consisted of sisters from the dioceses of Cloyne, Cork and Ross, Kerry and Limerick. This led to a significant change in the personnel in the Listowel convent. Until the 1970s the sisters were, with few exceptions, natives of Kerry diocese. Thereafter sisters in Listowel were transferred to other convents within the South West province and replaced by colleagues from those convents.

Another outcome of the renewal programme was the decision of some sisters 'to live among the people'. The sisters purchased a house in Ballygologue and three members of the community resided there from 1994 onwards.

The new focus on social activity was manifested in a number of ways. In 1986 a free laundry service for the elderly and others was opened in the convent. In 1991 the Presentation Sisters sited a Family Resource Centre in the former infants' school. Under the direction of Sister Gemma McGrath it assisted young mothers, early school-leavers, travellers and the marginalised of Listowel parish. Its education remit included parenting, personal development, household management and counselling. Initially the centre was funded by the sisters; later funding was secured from Kerry Educational Service, North Kerry Together Ltd, the St Vincent de Paul Society and the Southern Health Board. The range of services provided by the centre gradually increased as did the number of people attending. In 1997 the Department of Social, Community and Family Affairs refurbished the centre and in 1999 funding was granted by the department to enable it to continue and further extend its services to the community. The centre was re-named Presentation Family Centre Ltd and Sister Helen Dobbyn was given responsibility for its management. In 2001 the centre began offering computer courses. By then ten people were employed in the centre.

On 8 May 1994 the sisters celebrated the 150th anniversary of their arrival in Listowel. In her account of the celebrations Sister Sheilah Mary Ryan traced the history of the convent. She recalled the challenge faced by the sisters in the aftermath of the Famine:

> ... the 1840s proved to be years of the famine and fever which resulted in the deaths of so many, young and old, including some of the Sisters. In order to alleviate the distress suffered by so many families, the Sisters shared their own meagre and dwindling resources. In 1846 they trained their pupils to make, on contract with the workhouse, shirts for the male inhabitants and loose garments for the women for a few pence per garment. In 1847 the Sisters began to provide a breakfast for the starving children consisting of bread and a mug of boiled rice with a little milk. Soon the Sisters were feeding 250 daily. Over a period of twelve months 31,000 breakfasts had been supplied. But the following year the resources of the Sisters failed utterly and they had to rely on relief given by a Captain Sparks 'to the poor famishing Irish'. The Sisters were given for 400 children, a daily allowance of rye bread which was absolutely black: a loaf of which of eight, ten or twelve ounces was given according to the age of the recipient. The bread of absentees was given to expectant mothers ...

The greatest challenge which the sisters faced at the beginning of the third millennium was a very serious decline in vocations.

In the school year 2002-3, there were 16 teachers, including the principal Joan Mulvihill, and 260 pupils in the primary school and 40 teachers and 460 pupils in Meán Scoil Mhuire Fatima.[5] The special Nano Nagle school, where Bridie Murphy was principal, had 71 pupils. To care for these it had 10 full-time and 5 part-time teachers, 23 classroom assistants, a speech-therapist, a physiotherapist, a part-time occupational therapist, 2 social workers, a secretary and a caretaker. The Presentation community numbered fourteen, of whom ten had retired from teaching.[6]

NORTH KERRY PROGRAMME

This programme was initiated at 13 Upper William Street, Listowel, in June 2002. Under the aegis of Kerry Education Service and the Vocational Education Committee in Kerry, it was designed to deal with the effects of educational disadvantage in the area. The students were members of the Travelling Community and the settled community who did not have an adequate basic education in their youth. A variety of subjects were offered, including literacy, numeracy, art, crafts, design, drama, home management and personal development. Under the direction of Martina Hegarty, 26 students successfully completed the programme in 2002-3.[7]

5. For the principals of Presentation Secondary School: 1973-2003, see Appendix 2.
6. Convent diary, Presentation Convent, Listowel, and information from Sister Consolata Bracken.
7. Information from Martina Hegarty.

APPENDIX 1

Presidents and Teachers of St Michael's College: 1973–2003

Reverend Dermot O'Sullivan 1972–8
Reverend Patrick J. Horgan 1978–85
Reverend James Linnane 1985–9
Patrick Rochford 1989–92
John Mulvihill 1992–

✠ ✠ ✠

Ahern, Sheila 1990–
Bracken, Sister Consolata 1977–9
Brennan, Gabriel 1989–
Burke, John 1986–
Cody, Michael 1971–86
Cogan, Thomas J. 1973–
Crowley, Donncha 1981–94
Dillon, Conleth 1992–
Donovan, Louis 2002–
Donovan, Mary 1994–
Given, Patrick 1955–94
Greed, Ailish 1969–71
Griffin, Kieran 1980–1
Harmon, James C. 1968–
Hassett, Liam 2002–
Healy, Thomas 1981–
Heaphy, Morgan 2001
Horgan, Patrick J., Rev. 1978–85

Keane, Máire 1998–
Linnane, James, Rev. 1985-9
Lynch, Martin 1984–
McCarthy, Bryan 1979-80
Maloney, Philomena 1994–
Molyneaux, John 1953-90
Molyneaux, John J. 1968-2002
Moynihan, John D. 1975-2003
Mulcaire, Michael 1971–
Mulcahy, Sheila 1994–
Mulvihill, John 1992–
O'Brien, Brian F. 1970–
O'Donoghue, Mary 1992–
O'Flaherty, John 1972–
O'Regan, Joan 1972–
O'Regan, John 1972–
O'Sullivan, Brian 1979-80
O'Sullivan, Dermot Rev. 1972-8
Rochford, Patrick 1950-92
Rowley, Declan, 1987-8
Savage, Margaret 1972-3
Stack, Elizabeth 2002–
Toal, Inez 1986-9

APPENDIX 2

Principals of Presentation Secondary School: 1973–2003

Sister de Pazzi Lane 1945–74
Sister Eithne Casey 1974–81
Sister Eileen McCarthy 1981–3
Sister Sheila Kelleher 1983–6
Sister Consolata Bracken 1986–96
Tony Behan (acting-principal) 1996–7
Sister Nuala O'Leary 1997–

WRITERS

Those listed in Part I are creative writers whose work has been widely acclaimed. The authors in Part II have published valuable works which are the result of research and/or scholarship. The most important of these are the publications of Professors Pádraig de Brún, Máire Herbert and Cecile O'Rahilly.

Part I

Gabriel Fitzmaurice

Gabriel Fitzmaurice was born in Moyvane on 7 December 1952. He was educated at the local national school, St Michael's College and Mary Immaculate College of Education, Limerick. Following appointments in St Patrick's national school, Avoca, County Wicklow (1972-4) and Christ the King national school, Caherdavin, Limerick (1974-5), he began teaching in Moyvane national school in 1975, becoming principal in 2002.

He has served as chairman and literary adviser of Writers' Week, Listowel. A prolific author, he has published collections of poetry in English and Irish, collections of verse for children, translations from the Irish, collections of essays, songs and ballads and he has edited anthologies of poetry.

His publications include *Rainsong* (1984), *Road to the Horizon* (1987), *Dancing Through* (1990), *The Father's Part* (1992), *The Space Between: New and Selected Poems* (1984–1992), *The Village Sings* (1993), *A Wrenboy's Carnival: Poems* (1980-2000) and *I and the Village* (2002).

John B. Keane

John B. Keane was born in Listowel on 21 July 1928. His father was a schoolteacher and his mother a member of Cumann na mBan and a sister of Michael Purtill, one of the heroes of the Anglo-Irish war in North Kerry. He was educated at the local national school and St Michael's College. When he left college he began to serve his apprenticeship at Keane-Stack's pharmacy in Listowel. Shortly afterwards he emigrated to England where he worked at a variety of jobs. He returned to Ireland after two years and worked in Doneraile, County Cork, as a chemist's assistant. A year later he transferred to a similar post at Keane-Stack's, Listowel. Then early in 1955 he married and bought a public house in the town. He began to write plays and had several rejected by the Abbey Theatre. In 1959 came the great breakthrough. In that year's competition for the best amateur production in the country the Listowel Drama Group presented his play *Sive*. The Listowel group and Keane's play proved to be a winning combination. At the All-Ireland Drama Festival in Athlone the Listowel Drama Group and *Sive* won the premier awards for the best group and the best play.

Subsequently, John B. went from success to success, the

secret of which was his sheer dedication and untiring energy. He worked almost every night into the morning and consequently his output was enormous. He changed in no way with success, and remained refreshingly unassuming.

He published (for the most part his publisher was Mercier Press of Cork) *The Street and Other Poems* (1961), twenty collections of newspaper articles and short stories (1963-1999), a short autobiography, *Self-portrait* (1964), a biography, *Dan Pheadí Aindí* (in Irish 1977, in English 1984), a letter series which included *Letters of a Successful T.D.* (1969), *Letters of an Irish Parish Priest* (1972) and *Letters of an Irish Publican* (1974) and four novels, *The Bodhrán-makers* (1986), *Durango* (1992), *The Contractors* (1993) and *A High Meadow* (1994).

But it was as a playwright that he made his reputation and will be remembered. His published plays were *Sive* (1959), *Sharon's Grave* (1960), *The Highest House on the Mountain* (1961), *No More in Dust* (1962), *The Year of the Hiker* (1963), *The Field* (1966), *The Rain at the End of Summer* (1967), *Hut 42* (1968), *The Man from Clare* (1969), *Big Maggie* (1969), *Moll* (1971), *The Change in Mame Fadden* (1973), *Values* (a collection of three one-act plays) (1973), *The Crazy Wall* (1974), *The Good Thing* (1975), *The Buds of Ballybunion* (1976) and *The Chastitute* (1981). He completed two musicals, *Many Young Men of Twenty* (1961) and *The Roses of Tralee* (1966), and two other plays *Barbara Shearing* (1958) and *The One-way Ticket* (1972). *Faoiseamh*, a one-act play of his in Irish, won an award at the 1970 Oireachtas Drama Festival.

He was the most influential figure both in the establishment of Writers' Week, Listowel, and its subsequent success.

He died on 30 May 2002.

Brendan Kennelly

Another literary figure from the district is Brendan Kennelly. A second cousin of Bob Boland, he was born in Ballylongford on 17 April 1936. He was educated at the local national school and at St Ita's College, Tarbert. From 1955 to 1957 he was an ESB employee in Dublin. He then entered Trinity College, graduating in 1961. He continued at Trinity College and afterwards at Leeds University as a post-graduate student and obtained a PhD five years later. In 1963 he was appointed to the department of English in his *alma mater*, became a fellow of the college in 1967 and was promoted associate professor of English in 1969. Since 1973 he has been the occupant of the chair of modern literature and is a senior fellow of the college.

He published his first four books of poems, *Cast a Cold Eye* (1959), *The Dark About Our Loves* (1961), *The Rain, the Moon* (1962) and *Green Townlands* (1963), in conjunction with Rudi Holzapfel. In the decade following 1963 he published a further thirteen books of poems, entitled *Let Fall No Burning Leaf* (1963), *My Dark Fathers* (1964), *Up and At It* (1965), *Collection One: Getting Up Early* (1966), *Good Souls to Survive* (1967), *Dream of a Black Fox* (1968), *Selected Poems* (1969), *A Drinking Cup* (1970), *Bread* (1971), *Love Cry: the Kerry Sonnets* (1972), *Salvation, the Stranger* (1972), *Selected and New Poems* (1972), and *The Voices* (1973).

Between 1974 and 2003, he continued to be prolific, publishing: *Shelly in Dublin* (1974), *A Kind of Trust* (1975), *New and Selected Poems* (1976), *Islandman* (1977), *The Visitor* (1978), *A Small Light* (1979), *In Spite of the Wise* (1979), *The Boats are Home* (1980), *The House that Jack Didn't Build* (1979), *Cromwell: a Poem* (1983), *Moloney Up and At It* (1984), *Selected Poems* (1985), *Mary: from the Irish* (1987), *Love of Ireland: Poems from the Irish* (1989), *A Time for Voices:*

Selected Poems 1960-1990 (1990), *The Book of Judas: a Poem* (1991), *Breathing Spaces: Early Poems* (1992), *Poetry My Arse* (1995), *The Man Made of Rain* (1998), *The Singing Tree* (1998), *Begin* (1999), *Glimpses* (2001), *The Little Book of Judas* (2001) and *Martial Art* (2003).

Two novels by him, *The Crooked Cross* (1963) and *The Florentines* (1967), have been well received and were translated into Italian.

His plays, *Euripides' Medea* (1992), *Euripides' the Trojan Women* (1993), *Sophocles' Antigone* (1996) and *Lorca's Blood Wedding* (1996) were published by Bloodaxe Books of Newcastle upon Tyne.

He edited the *Penguin Book of Irish Verse* (1970) and a number of other anthologies.

His *Real Ireland* and *Ireland Past and Present* appeared in 1984 and 1985 respectively.

He has presided over a number of summer schools and poetry workshops. From its inception in 1971 he has been literary adviser to Writers' Week, Listowel, and he has written extensively for literary journals. In his honour the annual Brendan Kennelly Summer Festival was established in his native Ballylongford in 2000.

Bryan MacMahon

The versatile Bryan MacMahon was born in Listowel on 29 September 1909. He was educated in the local national school and at St Michael's College. Having trained as a teacher in St Patrick's College, Drumcondra, he returned to teach in Listowel national school from 1929 to 1974. A superb teacher, one would scarcely conceive of a more suitable person to whom to entrust the formation of the minds of the young as he had an edifying love of Ireland, its culture and its language.

He first came to prominence as a writer with a variety of contributions to *The Bell*, then edited by Seán Ó Faoláin. He also wrote poems for this magazine and Frank O'Connor welcomed him as a poet of quality. In 1945 his story, *The Good Dead in the Green Hills*, won The Bell Award and in 1948 his book of short stories, *The Lion Tamer*, was published in Britain and the United States. After a successful run with the Listowel Drama Group, of which he was a founding member, his play, *The Bugle in the Blood* was produced in the Abbey Theatre in March 1949. In 1950 he published, in the United States, a children's book, *Jackomoora and the King of Ireland's Son*. 1952 saw his novel *Children of the Rainbow* published in Britain, the United States and Canada. It was made a selection of The Book Find Club and also The Irish Book Club. Later it was translated into German and adapted for radio. Much of his work has been featured on the BBC as well as RTÉ. His second collection of short stories, entitled, *The Red Petticoat*, was published in 1955 and he had two plays, *Song of the Anvil* and *The Honey Spike*, produced by the Abbey Theatre in 1961 and 1962 respectively.

Commissioned by the GAA to write the pageant for the 1916 Jubilee Commemoration, he did not disappoint the organisers and his *Seachtar Fear: Seacht Lá* was very well received.

In 1967 he published *The Honey Spike*. This novel, which concerns itinerants, draws heavily on his considerable experience of and rapport with the 'travelling people'. In 1961 he collaborated in the publication of a children's schoolbook, *Brendan of Ireland*, and in 1970 he had another book for children, *Patsy-O and his Wonderful Pets*, published by Dutton. *Here's Ireland* and his translation of *Peig* appeared in 1971 and 1974 respectively.

Following his retirement he published further books for

children, *Patsy-O goes to Spain* (1989) and *Mascot Patsy-O* (1992), and collections of short stories, *The End of the World* (1976), *The Sound of Hooves* (1985), *The Tallystick* (1994) and *A Final Fling* (1998). *The Master*, an account of his life as a teacher, appeared in 1992 and *The Story Man*, a further volume of autobiography, was published in 1995.

During summer vacations he participated in literary seminars at a number of American universities. In his later years he was a cardinal figure in ensuring the success of Listowel's Writers' Week, not least by his presiding over 'writers' workshops' during the festival's early years. He continued to be an active supporter of amateur drama groups by whom *The Master* and his one-act plays, *The Time of the Whitethorn*, *The Gap of Life* and *Jack Furey* were presented.

In 1971 the National University conferred on him the doctorate of laws.

He died on 13 February 1998.

Part II

Daniel Boland

Daniel Boland was born in Farnastack, near Lisselton, on 1 January 1891. Like his older brother, Robert Leslie (Bob), the poet, he was educated at the local national school and St Michael's College.

After qualifying at King's College, London, he embarked on a distinguished legal career. He was first an officer and later an associate of the Supreme Court, London, from 1913 to 1915. In 1938 he became Secretary of the Masters of the Kings Bench Division and between then and his retirement in 1956 he held a number of important legal posts.

He gave his adopted country sterling service not only in the legal but also in the military field and was decorated for gallantry during World War I.

He received the MBE in 1949.

Although he contributed articles on diverse subjects to various magazines, his chief literary work consisted in his editing books which, for the most part, were only of interest to members of his own profession. The following is a list of some of these: *ABC Guide to the Practice of the Supreme Court* (1949 and 1953), *The Annual Practice of the Supreme Court* (1949-56), *Chitty's Queen's Bench Forms* (1956), *Civil Procedure in a Nutshell* (1956).

He died on 28 June 1973.

John Coolahan

John Coolahan was born in Tarbert on 9 June 1941. He was educated at the local national school, St Ita's College, St Patrick's College, Drumcondra, University College, Dublin, and Trinity College, Dublin.

After teaching in primary and secondary schools he was a lecturer in the department of education in University College, Dublin, from 1974 to 1987, when he was appointed to the chair of education in the National University of Maynooth, Ireland.

He edited *Irish Educational Studies* from 1980 to 1985 and has contributed numerous articles to specialist periodicals on education. From the 1990s onwards he has been much sought after as an adviser on education policy at national and international level.

His published works include *Irish Education: History and Structure* (1981) and *The ASTI and Post-primary Education in Ireland 1909-1984* (1984).

Padraig A. de Brún

Padraig A. de Brún was born in Listowel on 13 December 1940. He was educated at Lixnaw and Ballyduff national schools, Causeway Secondary School and University College, Cork.

In 1962-3 he was a member of the staff at St Patrick's College, Drumcondra. From 1963 to 1966 he was a lecturer in the Irish department of University College, Cork. In October 1966 he was appointed to the School of Celtic Studies in the Dublin Institute for Advanced Studies, where he became assistant professor in January 1972 and was professor and director of publishing from 1990 to 1998.

He was conferred with a DLitt by the National University of Ireland in 1977 and was honoured with membership of the Royal Irish Academy in 1994.

His MA thesis, which dealt with the Gaelic poets of north Kerry, prompted in him an interest in the local history of his own county and he edited the *Journal of the Kerry Archaeological and Historical Society* I-4 (1968-71) and 22 (1989). He co-edited *Celtica* 21 (1990) and 22 (1991) and, with Seán Ó Coileáin and Pádraig Ó Riain, edited *Folia Gadelica: Essays Presented by Former Students to R.A. Breatnach* (1983).

He has contributed numerous articles to *Éigse*, *Studia Hibernica* and other scholarly journals. His major works to date include: *Clár Lámhscríbhinní Gaeilge Choláiste Chorcaí: Cnuasach Thorna* (1967), *Catalogue of Irish Manuscripts in the Franciscan Library, Killiney* (1969), *Nua-Dhuanaire I* (1971, with B. Ó Buachalla and T. Ó Concheanainn), *Filíocht Sheáin Uí Bhraonáin* (1972) and *Catalogue of Irish Manuscripts in King's Inn Library, Dublin* (1972), *Catalogue of Irish Manuscripts in Cambridge Libraries* (1986; with Máire Herbert), *Lámhscríbhinní Gaeilge: Treoirliosta* (1988); and he edited *D.C. Hennessy, The Lays of North Kerry and Other Poems and Sketches* (2001).

A keen supporter of Kerry teams, he was a member of the historical committee writing the history of the GAA in the county and assisted Pat O'Shea to compile *Face the Ball: Records of the Kerry Senior Football and Hurling Championships 1889-1998* (1998).

Timothy Enright – Tadhg Mac Ionnrachtaigh

Timothy Enright was born on 7 February 1926. He was educated at the local national school, St Michael's College, and Trinity College, Dublin.

He emigrated to England in 1949, where he was a teacher in second-level schools until 1981. Active in left-wing politics, he joined the British Communist Party in 1955.

He was a close friend of the versatile scholar, George Thomson – Seoirse Mac Tomáis. They shared a deep and sympathetic understanding of the Irish language and culture, a love of the classics and an active commitment to Marxism and the British Communist Party.

Like Professor Thomson, Tim Enright was fascinated by the books written by the natives of the Blasket Islands. His English translation of a number of these for Oxford University Press were published as follows: Mícheál Ó Guiheen, *A Pity Youth Does Not Last*, together with a collection of poems from the same author, *Coinnle Corra: Wild Hyacinths* (1981); Tomás Ó Crohan, *Island Cross-talk: Pages from a Diary* (1986); and Seán Ó Crohan, *A Day in our Life* (1992).

He assisted George Thomson to complete his last book *Island Home: the Blasket Heritage* (1988), to which he appended a valuable memoir of his cherished friend.

Tim Enright died on 7 December 1993.

Máire Herbert

Máire Herbert was born in Ballyduff on 8 June 1948. She was educated at the local national school, Presentation Convent, Tralee, University College, Galway, Dublin Institute for Advanced Studies and University of Cambridge.

In 1974-8 she lectured in the Department of Old Irish, St Patrick's College, Maynooth. From 1978 onwards she has been a member of the staff of the Department of Early and Medieval Irish Language and Literature in University College, Cork, where she was appointed associate professor in 1993.

In the spring term 1986 she was guest lecturer in the Department of Anglo-Saxon, Norse and Celtic in the University of Cambridge, and in the academic year 1993-4 she was visiting professor in the Department of Celtic Languages and Literature in Harvard University. In 1996 she was honoured with membership of the Royal Irish Academy.

She has contributed numerous articles to a wide variety of literary and scholarly journals and periodicals. She edited *Saints and Scholars: Studies in Irish Hagiography* (2001; with J. Carey and P. Ó Riain), *Apocrypha Hiberniae: I. Evangelia Infantiae* (2001; with others) and *Prospect and Retrospect in Celtic Studies* (forthcoming; with K. Murray). Her major works are: *Catalogue of Irish Manuscripts in Cambridge Libraries* (1986; with Pádraig de Brún), I*ona, Kells and Derry: the History and Hagiography of the Monastic Familia of Columba* (1988), *Betha Adamnáin: the Irish life of Adamnan* (1988; with Pádraig Ó Riain) and *Irish Biblical Apocrypha: Selected Texts in Translation* (1989; with Martin McNamara).

Noel Kissane

Noel Kissane was born in Asdee on 26 November 1938. He was educated at Asdee national school, St Joseph's College, Freshford, County Kilkenny, and University College, Dublin. After teaching in a number of primary and post-primary schools he joined the staff of the National Library of Ireland in 1969. He served as Education Officer and Keeper of Manuscripts. As Education Officer, he made the National Library's collections accessible to schools and the general public through the medium of exhibitions and publications. He published twelve folders of facsimile documents for use in schools, which included *The Land War* (1976), *Daniel O'Connell* (1978), *Athbheochan na Gaeilge* (1981), *The G.A.A.* (1984) and *Historic Dublin Maps* (1988). He also published *Ex Camera* (1990), *Parnell: a Documentary History* (1991), *The Irish Famine: a Documentary History* (1995), and edited *Treasures of the National Library of Ireland* (1994). As Keeper of Manuscripts, he was mainly concerned with developing the National Library's collections and was involved in acquiring manuscripts of major significance, including the literary papers of W.B. Yeats, James Joyce, Séan O'Casey and Brian Friel, the Browne (Westport House) family archive, the Gormanston archive, and the Book of O'Hara, a volume of medieval bardic poetry. He retired in 2002.

Bryan M.E. McMahon

Bryan M.E. McMahon was born in Listowel on 10 April 1941. He was educated at the local national school, St Michael's College, University College, Dublin, and Harvard Law School.

From 1964 to 1966 he practised law. In 1966 he was a

lecturer in Mid-Essex College of Technology, Chelmsford, England. From 1967 to 1987 he was statutory lecturer and later professor of law in University College, Cork. And from 1987 to 1999 he was a partner in the law firm of Houlihan and McMahon, Ennis, County Clare, and held a part-time chair of law at University College, Galway. In 1999 he was appointed judge of the circuit court.

He was appointed to the Law Reform Commission in 1977, chairman of the National Crime Forum in 1998, chairman of the National Archive Advisory Council in 2003 and chairman of the Irish Universities Quality Board in 2003.

He has contributed articles, mainly on legal topics, to various journals. His major publications are: *Economic Law in Ireland* (1975), *Law of Torts* (with W. Binchy 1980), *European Community Law in Ireland* (with F. Murphy 1989), *Casebook on Irish Law of Torts* (with W. Binchy 1991), *Occupiers' Liability in Ireland: Survey and Proposals for Reform* (1994) and he has contributed to *Principles on European Contract Law I-III* (2003).

Father Francis X. Martin OSA

Francis X. Martin was born in Ballylongford on 2 October 1922. He was educated at Ring Irish college, Belvedere, University College, Dublin, Gregorian University (Rome) and Peterhouse, Cambridge. He entered the Augustinian order in 1941.

He was appointed a lecturer in the history department of University College, Dublin in 1959, and was professor of medieval history in the college from 1962 to 1990. In 1963 he was appointed a member of the Irish Manuscripts Commission. In 1967 he was elected a member of the Royal Irish Academy and in 1973 he became vice-chairman of the

Council of Trustees of the National Library of Ireland. As chairman of the Friends of Medieval Dublin (1976-83) he led the successful campaign to preserve and scientifically excavate the Viking and medieval archaeological site at Wood Quay.

With T.W. Moody he co-edited *The Course of Irish History* (1967, 1984) and with T.W. Moody and F.J. Byrne he co-edited *A New History of Ireland II-V, VIII-IX* (1976-89).

He published articles on medieval, Renaissance and counter-Reformation topics as well as on modern Irish history. Much of his work was connected with editing collections: *Medieval Studies Presented to Aubrey Gwynn, S.J.* (ed. J.A. Watt, J.B. Morrall and F.X. Martin) (1961), *The Irish Volunteers, 1913-15: Recollections and Documents* (ed. F.X. Martin) (1964), *The Howth Gunrunning, 1914: Recollections and Documents* (ed. F.X. Martin) (1964), *1916 and University College, Dublin* (ed. F.X. Martin) (1966), *Leaders and Men of the Easter Rising* (ed. F.X. Martin) (1967), and *The Scholar Revolutionary, Eoin MacNeill, 1867-1945, and the Making of the New Ireland* (ed. F.X. Martin and F.J. Byrne) (1973), and *Expugnatio Hibernica: the Conquest of Ireland* (ed. F.X. Martin and A.B. Scott) (1978). In 1960 and 1962 he published *Giles of Viterbo, 1469-1532, Humanist and Reformer* and *Friar Nugent: a Study of Francis Lavalin Nugent, 1569-1653, Agent of the Counter-Revolution*, respectively.

He died on 13 February 2000.

Father Malachi B. Martin SJ

Malachi B. Martin was born in Ballylongford on 23 July 1921. He was educated at Ring Irish college, Belvedere College, University College, Dublin, and the University of Louvain.

He entered the Society of Jesus in 1939 and was

ordained in 1954. In 1958-9 he was a member of the staff in the Jesuit House of Formation, Milltown Park. From 1959 to 1961 he lectured at the Pontifical Biblical Institute in Rome, where he was professor of palaeontology and Semitic languages from 1961 to 1964.

He left the Jesuits and the active priesthood in 1965 and settled in New York. He published: *The Pilgrim* (1964), *The Scribal Characters of the Dead Sea Scrolls I-II* (1969), *The Encounter* (1969), *Three Popes and the Cardinal* (1972), *Jesus Now* (1974), *The New Castle* (1974), *Hostage to the Devil* (1976), *The Final Conclave* (1978), *King of Kings* (1980), *Decline and Fall of the Roman Church* (1984), *There is Still Love* (1984), *Rich Church, Poor Church* (1984), *Vatican* (1986), *The Jesuits* (1987), *The Keys of the Blood* (1990) and *Windswept house – a Vatican Novel* (1996).

He died on 27 July 1999.

John Moriarty

John Moriarty was born in Moyvane on 2 February 1938. He was educated at the local national school, St Michael's College, St Patrick's College, Drumcondra, University College, Dublin, and the University of Leeds.

He lectured in the English department of the University of Manitoba, Canada, from 1965 to 1971.

Following his return to Ireland he embraced the intellectual life almost like a religious vocation. He sought solitude in Connemara (1971-1993) and at Mangerton, near Killarney (1995-2003).

A profound thinker, his writing is highly regarded and he is a popular lecturer.

He has published: *Dreamtime* (1994), *Turtle was Gone a Long Time I: Crossing the Kedron* (1996), *Turtle was Gone a Long Time II: Horsehead Nebula Neighing* (1997), *Turtle was*

Gone a Long Time III: Anaconda Canoe (1998) and *Nostos* (2001).

An tAthair Mícheál Ó Ciosáin

Mícheál Ó Ciosáin was born in Ballydonoghue on 16 October 1920. He was educated at the local national school, St Michael's College, St Brendan's Seminary, Killarney, and St Patrick's College, Maynooth.

He was ordained for the diocese of Kerry in 1946. He ministered in the archdiocese of Cardiff from 1946 to 1948. On his return to his own diocese he was chaplain to Edenburn hospital from 1948 to 1951. Thereafter he was a curate in the parish of Ballyferriter from 1951 to 1967 and its parish priest from 1967 to 1989. He was tireless in his efforts to ensure that the Irish language and culture continued to flourish in Ballyferriter and the rest of the West Kerry Gaeltacht.

A keen historian, he edited *Céad Bliain: 1871-1971* in 1973 and published *Cnoc an Fhomhair* in 1989.

He died on 15 July 1991.

Seán O'Quigley

Seán O'Quigley was born in Listowel on 3 December 1914. He was educated at the local national school, St Michael's College, Blackrock College and University College, Dublin.

In 1940, after qualifying in medicine, he joined the defence forces and served at Baldonnell with the Air Corps and subsequently in St Bricín's Military Hospital. He was a member of the Irish army contingent which served under the United Nations in the Lebanon in 1958. In 1960 he was appointed chief medical officer in Aer Lingus. He retired in 1979.

Dr O'Quigley served as a member, vice-president and president of a number of international and national associations and committees concerned with aviation, occupational and space medicine.

He published *Health and Travel* in 1979.

He died on 6 March 1994.

Cecile O'Rahilly

Cecile O'Rahilly, sister of Alfred and Thomas F., was born in Listowel on 17 December 1894. She received her early education at the local Presentation Convent School and Dominican College, Eccles Street, Dublin. In 1912 she entered University College, Dublin, and, like her brothers, had a distinguished academic career. She graduated in 1915 with a double first in Celtic Studies and French and the following year she won a travelling studentship in Celtic Studies. This she held in the University College of North Wales, Bangor, where she obtained her MA in 1919.

From 1919 to 1928 she taught French in Beaumaris Grammar School in Anglesey and later, from 1928 to 1946, held a similar post in Cardiff High School for Girls. In 1946 she was appointed an assistant professor and in 1956 professor in the school of Celtic Studies of the Dublin Institute for Advanced Studies. She retired in 1964.

Her major publications are: *Gruaidhe Griansholus* (1924), *Ireland and Wales: their Historical and Literary Relations* (1924), *Five Seventeenth-century Political Poems* (1949), *Eachtra Uilliam* (1952), *Stowe Version of Táin Bó Cuailnge from the Book of Leinster* (1967) and *Táin Bó Cuailnge: Recension I* (1976).

She died on 2 May 1980.

Brendan O'Shea

Brendan O'Shea was born in Listowel on 6 January 1943. He was educated at the local national school, St Michael's College, University College, Galway, London University and the University of Nebraska. After lecturing in the University of Leeds from 1970 to 1971, he joined the staff of the Dublin Institute of Technology, where he is now head of the School of Computer Science. He has been a frequent contributor to journals on computer science.

He was the Irish marathon champion in 1973, he represented Ireland in international marathons and was the national coach for distance runners from 1984 to 1989. With Ann Barry and John P. Kevany, he co-authored *Food for Sport and Fitness* in 1983.

Father Kieran O'Shea

Kieran O'Shea was born in Listowel on 13 April 1937. He was educated at the local national school, St Michael's College and St Brendan's Seminary, Killarney. He entered St Patrick's College, Maynooth, in 1954 and was ordained for the diocese of Kerry in 1961.

From 1961 to 1963 he ministered in the diocese of Nottingham and from 1963 to 1967 he was a member of the Irish Chaplaincy Scheme in England and was based in Luton and Birmingham. After his return to his diocese in 1967 he served in the parishes of Eyeries, Causeway and Castleisland. From 1968 to 1975 he was chaplain to Causeway Comprehensive School. He was appointed parish priest of Knocknagoshel in 1990.

Apart from the issue of 1989, he edited the journals of the Kerry Archaeological & Historical Society from 1972 to 1993. He published *Castleisland: Church and People* (1981),

The Irish Emigrant Chaplaincy Scheme in Britain 1957-82, (1985), *Knocknagoshel Parish* (1991) and valuable articles on Bishops David Moriarty and Rickard O'Connell. In 1985 he co-edited *Listowel and the GAA 1885-1985*. Since 1997 he has been chairman of the historical committee, writing the history of the GAA in Kerry. In this role with Pádraig de Brún, he assisted Pat O'Shea to compile *Face the Ball: Records of the Kerry Senior Football and Hurling Championships 1889-1998* (1998).

Robert Pierse

Robert Pierse was born in Listowel on 31 December 1937.

He was educated at the local national school, St Michael's College and University College, Dublin.

He qualified as a solicitor in 1960 and two years later established the immensely successful firm which became Pierse and Fitzgibbon solicitors in 1975. A regular contributor to legal journals, he published *Road Traffic Law in the Republic of Ireland* in 1989 and *The Quantum of Damages in Personal Injury Cases in Ireland* in 1997.

MORE WRITERS

Those listed in Part I are creative writers whose work is little known beyond North Kerry. Those in Part II have published autobiography and local history. In Part III is a list of journalists from the area.

PART I

Maureen Beasley

Maureen Horgan was born on 19 May 1918 in Killocrim, Listowel. She was educated at Listowel's Presentation Convent School and Dromclough national school.

She married Johnny Beasley in 1948.

A rhymer from the earliest years, she had poems published in various magazines and periodicals. She presided over Poet's Corner at Writers' Week for many years. A collection of her poems, *The Homes of Killocrim*, was published in 1989.

Michael J. Costello

Michael J. Costello was born near Causeway on 21 April 1939. He was educated at Killahan national school.

He spent much of his life working abroad, first in England and later in the US.

He published a number of slim books of poetry among which were: *Shadows in the Valley* (1993), *Down Memory Lane* (1995), *Famous People* (1995), *From Earth to Heaven* (1995), *Through the Years. A North Kerry Boyhood* (1998) and *The Green Leaves of Summer* (2001).

He died on 29 September 2002.

William (Bill) Dee

William Dee was born in Listowel on 3 June 1965.

He was educated at Lisselton national school, Vocational School, Listowel, Regional Technical College, Cork, and the Open University, London.

From 1986 to 1987 he was a quality controller at the Food Centre at Raheen, Limerick. In 1987 he emigrated and from then to 1996 he was a member of the staff of Thomas Watson, where, eventually, he was promoted to the post of Senior Microbiologist for London's drinking water. From 1996 to 1999 he was a consultant in the educational sector. In 1999 he became deputy director of the National Listening Library and was promoted director in 2001. This organisation provides audio books for people across the UK who have print impairments (visual impairments, physical difficulties with holding a book or learning difficulties).

In the meantime, in 1999, Bill founded Prendeville Publishing Ltd. which issues books on subjects of Irish interest.

In 1983 he won a prize for his poetry at Writers' Week.

In the millennium year he began to write poetry again and in 2001 won the 'Golden Pen' prize.

A number of his poems were published in *Humble Beginnings* in 1986.

Patrick Fitzgibbon

Patrick Fitzgibbon was born in Listowel on 7 January 1945.

He was educated at the local national school, Newbridge College, County Kildare, and University College, Dublin.

After completing his legal studies he practised in Listowel from 1968 onwards. He has been a partner in the firm Pierse and Fitzgibbon solicitors since 1975.

He published a play *Estuary* in 1993 and a collection of poems *A Memo to Ringelblum and Other Poems* in 2001.

Patrick Given

Patrick Given was born in Knock, County Mayo, on 25 February 1934. Four years later his family moved to Listowel where he was educated at the local national school and St Michael's College. From 1951 to 1955 he attended University College, Galway.

He was on the staff of St Michael's from 1955 to 1994.

His literary work to date consists of *The King's Servant* (a play on the life of St Thomas More broadcast by Radio Éireann in 1961), *Poems* (1967) and *Pilgrimage Along the Feale* (collection of poems 1976).

Tony Guerin

Tony Guerin was born in Listowel on 23 August 1938. He was educated at the local national school and St Michael's

College. He served in the Garda Síóchána from 1963 to 1994.

His plays *Cuckoo Blue* (1998) and *Solo Run* (2002) have been produced by the Lartigue Theatre Company of Listowel and *Hummin'* (2002) was presented by the Red Kettle Theatre Company of Waterford.

Denis C. (D.C.) Hennessy[1]

Denis C. Hennessy was born in Listowel about 1842. He attended the local national school. In 1872 he published a book of sixty-six poems entitled *The Lays of North Kerry, and Other Poems and Sketches.*

A remarkable man by any standards, he earned his living from a small newspaper shop (situated in Lower William Street) and by attending the sittings of the county court and supplying reports to the local provincial newspaper. The first-hand information he so acquired probably inspired his poem, 'Our County Courts and Rural J.P.s', which casts a jaundiced eye on those locally entrusted with the administration of the law.

He encouraged a number of Listowel men to take up careers in journalism: E.T. Keane, John A. O'Sullivan and Thomas F. O'Sullivan. While E.T. Keane was still a student in St Michael's College he attended court sittings with Hennessy and, as the latter's sight was seriously impaired, helped him to file his newspaper reports.

From his poems one gathers that he was a staunch nationalist and a devout Catholic. One also learns that his brother 'joined a patriot band', was betrayed by a traitor' and sent to jail and 'an early death'.

---

1. Hennessy is included here because of information in Pádraig de Brún's new edition in 2001 of the collection of his poems.

Hennessy, who is traditionally referred to as 'the blind poet of north Kerry', had lost his sight some years before he died of tuberculosis on 23 April 1884.

Daniel Keane

Daniel Keane was born at Carrueragh, Moyvane, on 17 September 1919. He was educated at Knockanure national school.

He was a farm worker from 1932 to 1946 and an insurance representative from 1947 to 1984.

Steeped in the lore of the North Kerry countryside, his poetry has been published extensively in journals and magazines.

His *The Heather is Purple, a Collection of Poems*, appeared in 1986.

Eamon Kelly

Eamon Kelly was born in Rathmore, County Kerry, on 30 March 1914. Soon afterwards his family transferred to Killarney where he was educated at Lissivigeen national school. After spending a few years apprenticed to his father as a carpenter, he was persuaded to attend Killarney Technical School. Eventually he trained as a woodwork teacher. In this capacity he was a member of the staff of Waterville Technical School from 1939 to 1941 and Listowel Technical School from 1943 to 1952.

In Listowel Eamon Kelly was an active member of the Listowel Drama Group and married another active member, Maura O'Sullivan in 1951. They continued to perform in amateur drama productions. Then from 1952 to 1964 they were members of the Radio Éireann Repertory Company. Later between 1967 and 1999 Eamon occasionally acted in productions by the Abbey Theatre.

Eamon Kelly was a unique interpreter of the Seanchaí tradition of storytelling and was renowned for his one man shows.

His novels *The Apprentice* and *The Journeyman* were published in 1995 and 1998 respectively.

He died on 24 October 2001.

Patrick Kennelly

Patrick Kennelly, brother of Brendan, was born in Ballylongford on 18 February 1946. He was educated at the local national school, St Ita's College, Tarbert (1958-9) and St Brendan's Seminary, Killarney.

Between 1963 and 1965 he trained as a primary school teacher at St Patrick's College, Drumcondra, and later taught at St Brendan's national school, Coolock, Dublin. He taught at Duagh national school from 1969 to 1972 and at Asdee national school from 1972 to 2001.

He published his novel *Sausages for Tuesday* in 1969 and *A Place too Small for Secrets* in 2002.

John McAuliffe

John McAuliffe was born in Roscommon on 14 May 1973. His family settled in Listowel in 1984 and he completed his primary education at Scoil Réalta na Maidne. He was subsequently educated at St Michael's College, University College, Galway, Southern Illinois University at Carbondale and Trinity College, Dublin. From 1998 onwards he was a teacher and tutor in a number of colleges and universities. In 2002 he was appointed head of English to Albemarle Independent College, London, and part-time lecturer on creative writing at Birbeck College, University College, London.

A frequent contributor to literary magazines and periodicals he is literary editor of *Cúirt Annual* and contributing editor to the poetry magazine *Metre*. His first collection of poems *A Better Life* was published in 2002.

Seán McCarthy

Seán McCarthy was born in Listowel on 5 July 1923. He was educated in the local national school. From 1937 to 1939 he worked on a number of farms in the vicinity of the town. In 1939 he joined the British army, was later wounded in action in the Middle East and, finally, was demobilised in 1946. Between 1946 and 1957 he travelled all over Ireland, England, Scotland and Wales as a folk singer with The Weavers. Thereafter, he composed numerous ballads, some of which were sung by Ireland's leading ballad singers. In 1970 he settled in Greenville, South Carolina, where he worked as a journalist and contributed to radio and television programmes. In 1974 he returned to Listowel, wrote a column for the *Kerryman* and took part in radio programmes.

He published *Book of Ballads* (1966), *Wanderings of a Lonely Man* (1968), *Darling Kate and Other Poems* (1972), *Songs of Seán McCarthy* (1973), *The Golden Bell of Obh-la-Lee* (n.d.), *The Road to Song* (n.d.), *A Dream of Christmas* (n.d.) and *I Never Saw a Purple Cow* (1987).

He died on 1 November 1990.

Patrick O'Connor

Patrick O'Connor was born in Listowel on 24 July 1919. He received his early education at Listowel national school and St Michael's College. In 1940 he entered University College, Cork, and graduated in 1943.

He was on the teaching staff of St Flannan's College, Ennis, from 1944 to 1956, Sandymount High School from 1956 to 1958 and Blackrock College from 1958 to 1988. While in Ennis he co-founded the Ennis Drama Group.

His first literary efforts consisted of collaboration work with Bryan MacMahon and Michael Kennelly in the light comedies, *Fledged and Flown* (1946) and *The Cobweb's Glory* (1947). From 1956 onwards he wrote extensively as a theatre and film critic. From 1956 to 1969, under the pseudonym L.S. Tuathaíl, he was theatre and film critic for *Comhar* and from 1959 to 1961, under the pseudonym Conor Sweeney, he was theatre correspondent for Radio Éireann. He was drama critic for *The Furrow* from 1961 to 1968. From 1965 to 1973 he was film critic and book reviewer for *Hibernia* and from 1969 to 1975 television critic of *The Standard*. In the 1980s and 1990s he was film critic for the *Sunday Tribune* and the *RTÉ Guide* magazine. Throughout his life he contributed numerous short stories and articles to various magazines and newspapers.

He died on 31 March 1996.

Father Cornelius O'Keeffe

Cornelius O'Keeffe was born in Kilmorna, near Listowel, on 17 November 1929. He attended Asdee national school, Rockwell College and St Brendan's Seminary, Killarney. He continued his studies at Holy Cross College, Clonliffe, University College, Dublin, and St Patrick's College, Maynooth. In 1955 he was ordained for the archdiocese of Dublin where he ministered until his final illness two years before he died on 24 February 1999. He was a member of the group of Dublin priests who from 1962 onwards produced and presented the successful series of *Radharc* programmes on RTÉ.

Father O'Keeffe was keenly interested in rural drama and founded the Asdee Players for whom he wrote a one-act play: *The Later Days are Cold* (1960). Another one-act play of his, *The Survivors* (1963) was presented by the Brosna Players. However, it is for his work in collecting the ballads and folklore of north Kerry and in ensuring the preservation of much of the latter in his publication, the *Shannonside Annual* (1956-60, that he will be remembered.

Christian O'Reilly

Christian O'Reilly was born in London on 24 November 1968 but was raised in Listowel. He was educated at the local national school, St Michael's College and Dublin City University.

His short stories have been published in a number of magazines.

A professional scriptwriter, his work has been produced on radio, television, in film and in the theatre. He is best known for his plays, *It Just Came Out* (2000) and *The Good Father* (2002).

Séamus Wilmot

A first cousin of Joe O'Connor, Séamus Wilmot was born in Listowel on 4 May 1902. He was educated at the local national school, St Michael's College and later at University College, Cork, where he graduated in commerce in 1922. There followed a succession of teaching appointments – five years at St Michael's College, three years at Belvedere College, Dublin, and one year at Rathmines Technical School. In 1931 he was appointed chief executive officer (CEO) of the County Wexford Vocational Education Committee and while in that post opened the first rural vocational school in Ireland at Camolin in 1932. He left Wexford to become town clerk of Galway in 1935. During his term of office the ancient corporation of the city was restored by the Local Government Act of 1937.

A lifelong devotee of the Irish language, he played a major role in building up Galway's unique Gaelic theatre, An Taibhdhearc. After three years in Galway he took up an appointment in Dublin as chief clerk of the National University. He became registrar in 1952 (he retired in 1972) and in July 1953 was awarded the university's doctorate of laws. He was one of the founders of Compántas Amharclanna na Gaeilge, which for some ten years produced a popular, bi-lingual variety show in every theatre in Dublin.

His writings stemmed from his dual concern with the Irish language and the theatre. He had ten plays in Irish produced and published.

He wrote two novels, one in Irish entitled *Mise Meara* (1946) and the other in English, an autobiographical one, entitled *The Splendid Pretence* (1947). A collection of short stories of his, *Eochair na Sráide*, was published by An Gúm in 1968, and *And So Began*, adapted from *Mise Meara*, was published in 1973.

He was a director of the Abbey Theatre from 1958 to 31 January 1974 and continued to have an absorbing interest in Irish drama, both amateur and professional. On 9 February 1974 to 31 January 1974 he was appointed chairman of the Folk Theatre (Siamsa Tíre).

He died on 28 January 1977.

1. A gold box from Ballinclemesig, late Bronze Age 700–800 BC. Was probably a gold ear spool.

2. Listowel Parish Pastoral Council 2002-3. *Front row (l-r)*: Canon James Linnane, Kay Kennelly, Fr John Kerin CC, and Patrick O'Sullivan (chairman). *Back row (l-r)*: Jackie McGillicuddy, Mairéad O'Sullivan, Owen McMahon, Mary O'Connor, Fr James Linehan CC, Cora Loughnane and Marie Breen.

3. Listowel Town Council after 1979 local election. *Standing (l-r):* Michael Barrett, Robert Pierse, Maria O'Gorman, John Holly, Tony O'Callaghan, Thomas P. Walsh and Michael O'Neill. *Seated (l-r):* William Walsh (town engineer), Thomas F. Collins (county manager), Albert Kennedy (chairman) and William Wixted (town clerk). Missing: Gerard Lynch.

4. Kerry Group plc Executive Directors:
   Top left: Hugh Friel, CEO, Kerry Group plc
   Top right: Denis Cregan, Deputy CEO, Kerry Group plc and CEO, Kerry Ingredients
   Middle left: Stan McCarthy, President and CEO, Kerry Ingredients Americas
   Middle right: Flor Healy, CEO, Kerry Foods
   Left: Brian Mehigan, CFO, Kerry Group plc

5. Listowel Presentation Sisters in 1994 on the occasion of the celebration of the 150th anniversary of the establishment of the convent. *Sitting (l-r)*: Sr Edmund, Sr Colette, Sr Thomas, Sr Therese, Sr Clare and Sr Carmel. *Standing (l-r)*: Sr Consolata, Sr Anne, Sr Sheilah Mary, Sr Philomena, Sr Marina, Sr Gemma, Sr Elizabeth, Sr Dympna, Sr de Pazzi, Sr Carmelita, Sr Kathleen and Sr Cyril.

6. Gabriel Fitzmaurice at the launching of his first book, *Rainsong*, Writers' Week, 1984. *L-R*: Fr J. Anthony Gaughan (President, Writers'Week), Gabriel Fitzmaurice and Bryan MacMahon.

7. Prof. Máire Herbert in 2003.   8. Katie Hannon in 2004.

9. Imbolc: the festival of spring. One of a series of four panels depicting the major festivals of the Celtic year. These works in copper by Tony O'Callaghan were commissioned for the Central Bank of Ireland in 1979.

Imbolc is associated with spring, with the goddess Brigit and a sacred flame which purifies the land and encourages fertility. Until recent times a vague ritual called the 'capall,' related to horse sacrificing, was practised in south Kerry on 1 February.

10. Members of the Listowel branch of Comhaltas Ceoltóirí Éireann in the old market yard before setting out 'on the wren' to raise funds for the Old Folks Home, St Stephen's Day, 1968. *Front row (l-r)*: Maurice Mahony, Michael Dowling, Timothy Brosnan, Mick Regan and Christy Stack. *Second Row (l-r)*: Anne Sayers and Babe Jo Wilmot. *Back row (l-r)*: Tim Leahy, Eamon Keane, Jack Larkin (above Babe Jo Wilmot), Maurice Kennelly, John Pierse and Tim Nolan.

11. Danny Hannon, founder of the Lartigue Theatre and Lartigue Theatre Company, with the cast of the company which presented *The Communication Cord* at St John's Theatre and Arts Centre in 2004. *Standing (l-r)*: Danny Hannon (director), Dolores O'Carroll, Elizabeth Stack, Con Kirby, Denis O'Mahony (producer) and Mike Moriarty. *Sitting (l-r)*: Jerry Hannon, Cathy Healy, Tommy Deenihan and Laura Shine.

12. Colm O'Brien, director of the Listowel Singers, with Pope John
    Paul II. The group travelled to Rome in 1989 to sing High Mass in
    St Peter's Basilica. They also performed a number of concerts in
    Rome including a concert in the Irish College, attended by
    Cardinal Tomás Ó Fiaich. At a private audience with the pope they
    sang a selection of Irish songs.

13. Staff of the Seanchaí – Kerry Literary and Cultural Centre 2004.
(L-R): Margaret Histon, Noreen Pattwell, Kathy Toolan and Cara
Trant. The picture is taken outside the centre with the background
of an art mural painted by local second level students.

14. Writers' Week Committee 2002: *Front row (l-r):* Máire Logue, Bill Walsh, Sheila Barry, Dan Keane, David Browne, Joanna Keane O'Flynn, Eilish Wren, Madeleine O'Sullivan, Mary Kennelly. *Back row (l-r):* Tony Guerin, Rose Wall, Cara Trant, John McGrath, Miriam O'Brien, Denise McKenna, Sean Broderick, Fiona Morvan, Margaret Broderick, Siobhán Stack, Deirdre O'Brien, Peter Given, Linda Galvin and Elaine Kinsella.

15. *L-R:* Tim Kennelly, John O'Flaherty, John Molyneaux, Páidí Ó Sé and Jimmy Deenihan. Kennelly, Deenihan and Ó Sé captained All-Ireland-winning football teams in 1979, 1981 and 1985 respectively. They developed their skills at St Michael's College, where Molyneaux and O'Flaherty trained teams between 1953 and 2000.

16. The Friends of Maurice Walsh Memorial Group, 1992. *Front row (l-r):* Betty Hartnett (treasurer), Chriss Nolan (chairperson and PRO), Kit Ahern (secretary). *Back row (l-r):* Jack Walsh, Margaret Gilbert, Maureen Nolan and John Foran.

17. John Binning (1812-1899), first settler (1852) in the place in the 'Queen's Bush' which became Listowel, Ontario, Canada.

18. A watercolour of Ballinruddery House, the only known representation of the house in existence, painted in the early to mid-nineteenth century. For more on Ballinruddery House, see p.167.

PART II

Gerry Allman

Gerry Allman was born at Rockfield, Faha, Milltown, County Kerry, on 24 May 1905. He was educated at the local national school, St Brendan's Seminary, Killarney, Presentation Brothers School, Killarney, and De La Salle Training College, Waterford.

Between 1925 and 1934 he taught in national schools first in Birr, County Offaly, and later in Tralee. From 1934 to 1939 he was a member of the staff of the Cashen national school, Ballyduff, and from 1939 to 1972 he was principal of Killury national school, Causeway. He served as president of the Irish National Teachers Organisation in 1967-8.

His *Causeway, Co Kerry: its Location, Lore and Legend* was published in 1983.

He died on 17 September 1983.

Vincent Carmody

Vincent Carmody was born in Listowel on 16 November 1944.

He was educated at the local national school, St Michael's College and the Vocational School.

He has been a Post Office employee in Listowel since 1969.

A keen local historian, he co-edited *Listowel and the GAA 1885-1985* in 1985 and published *North Kerry Camera: Listowel and its Surroundings (1860-1960)* in 1989.

John Dennehy

John Dennehy was born in Duagh on 27 June 1946.

He was educated at the local national school, St Michael's College, St Patrick's College, Drumcondra, University College, Dublin, Trinity College, Dublin, and Harvard University.

Between 1966 and 1972 he was a member of the staff of St Gabriel's national school, Aughrim St, Dublin; Scoil Mhuire, Blakestown, Clonsilla, Dublin; and St Assam's boys national school, Raheny, Dublin. He was principal of Scoil Cholmcille, Ballybrack, County Dublin, from 1972 to 1978. He became an inspector of schools in 1978 and was appointed assistant chief inspector in 1993.

In this last capacity he had special responsibility for the teaching of the arts in primary schools. To this end he published a wide range of books and teachers' manuals on the teaching of the visual arts in primary schools. Among these were: *Art and Crafts in the Primary School* (1969, with Liam Curran), *Craft Activities in the Primary School* (1970) and *More Craft Activities in the Primary School* (1972).

In 1998, after serving for two years as assistant secretary, he was appointed secretary general of the Department of Education and Science. From 1995 onwards he represented the department on the Education Committee of the Organisation for Economic Co-operation and Development (OECD) and in 2000 he was elected its chairman.

Michael Guerin

Michael Guerin was born in Listowel on 6 February 1946. He was educated at the local national school, St Michael's College and the Vocational School. Since 1962 he has been an employee of the ESB. He has had a life-long interest in the Lartigue railway and published *The Lartigue: Listowel and Ballybunion Railway* in 1988. He published *Listowel Workhouse Union* in 1996.

Kathleen (Kath) Hardie, *née* Cleary

Kathleen Cleary was born in London on 18 January 1932.

She was raised at Ballyline, Ballylongford, where she attended the local national school. Subsequently she was educated at the Presentation Convent Secondary School, Listowel, Coláiste Íde, Dingle, and University College, Galway.

She was a member of the staff of the Vocational School, New Inn, County Galway (1954-6), Vocational School, Portlaoise (1956-8) and Loyola College, Ibadan, Nigeria (1959-63). She married David Hardie in 1963.

Subsequent teaching appointments followed at Kitwe Girls High School, Zambia (1966-9), as training officer in Nchanga Inc. Copper Mines, Zambia (1969-73), St Modan's High School, Scotland (1976-81) and Denny High School, Scotland (1981-91).

She is a frequent contributor to newspapers and magazines and has had plays broadcast on RTÉ and Radio Scotland. She published *Was Your Mother's Name Jocasta?*, a collection of her work, in 1997, and *Sir Walter Scott: an Illustrated Historical Guide* in 2001.

Luke Keane

Luke Keane was born in Knocknagoshel in 29 September 1940. He was educated at the local national school and thereafter worked on the family farm.

For many years he has been the local correspondent for the *Kerryman* and the *Limerick Leader* and has published *Knocknagoshel, Then and Now* annually since 1984.

Collette Nunan Kenny

Collette Nunan Kenny was born in Moyvane on 25 December 1941.

She was educated at the local national school, Mercy Convent, Spanish Point, County Clare, Mercy Convent, Limerick and London College of Music and Drama.

A teacher of speech and drama, she has contributed to radio and television programmes on RTÉ and is a regular contributor to Radio Kerry.

She has published *Box of Words* (1984), *Earth Woman* (1986) and *Mule to Mercedes* (1994).

David Kissane

Born in Lisselton on 21 July 1953, David Kissane was educated at the local national school, St Michael's College, University College, Cork, and University College, Dublin. A member of the staff of St Paul's College in Raheny, Dublin, from 1976 to 1983, since then he has been teaching in the Comprehensive School, Tarbert. He edited the *Ballydonoghue Parish Magazine* from 1990 to 1998 and published *Kerry Community Games – a 21 year History* in 1993 and *Wings on Their Feet. A Story of Kerry B.L.E. 1967-1998* in 1998.

Timothy Leahy

Timothy Leahy was born on 29 January 1927 at Clounmacon. He was educated at the local national school and St Michael's College. He joined the Garda Síochána in 1946. After serving at a number of stations throughout the country, he was appointed superintendent in charge of the Buncrana district in 1967 and later transferred to Kilrush, where he retired in 1990. He published *Memoirs of a Garda Superintendent* in 1996.

Patrick Lysaght

Patrick Lysaght was born in Limerick on 15 May 1917. He spent his early years in Duagh and was educated at the local national school, St Michael's College, the Crescent College, Limerick, and All Hallows College, Dublin.

From 1937 to 1947 he was a member of the staff of O'Mahony's bookshop in Limerick. Then he emigrated to England, where he was employed at Ducketts, the book publishers and booksellers on the Strand in London. For several years he edited *Duckett's Register*. In 1963 he returned to Ireland and joined the family business in Limerick, The Treaty Printing Company, from which he retired in 1986.

A book-lover and keen historian, he published *Patron Saints* (1963), *Notes Towards a History of Duagh* (1970), *Comic History of Limerick* (1979), *Comic History of Kerry* (1981), *Irish Literary Quiz Book* (1984), *How to Become a Successful TD* (1987), *The River Feale* (1987) and *A Torrent of Versatile Verses* (2001).

Michael McCarthy

Michael McCarthy was born in Listowel on 20 April 1918. He was educated at the local national school.

After a number of business ventures, he became proprietor of The Embankment in Tallaght where he also promoted professional singing groups.

He published two volumes of autobiography *Early Days* and *London Years* in 1990. His play *The Rape of Dublin* (1996) was presented professionally.

He died on 4 April 2004.

Bryan MacMahon

Bryan MacMahon was born in Ballyheigue on 2 September 1949.

He was educated at the local national school, Christian Brothers School, Tralee, St Brendan's Seminary, Killarney, University College, Cork, and St Patrick's College, Kiltegan.

He was a teacher in a mission school in Kitui, Kenya from 1974 to 1975, a member of the staff of the Christian Brothers School, Kilcock, from 1977 to 1980 and has been teaching in Cabinteely Community School since 1980. He published *The Story of Ballyheigue* in 1994 and is a frequent contributor to historical journals.

John Molyneaux

John Molyneaux was born in Listowel on 9 April 1930. He was educated at the local national school, St Michael's College and University College, Galway.

He was a member of the staff of De La Salle College, Wicklow, from 1952 too 1953 and St Michael's College from 1953 to 1990.

He edited *Clár Cuimhne, 1898-1960, Páirc na h-Imeartha, Lios Tuathail* (1960) and *Páirc Mhic Shíthigh, Lios Tuathail* (1981), and co-edited *Listowel and the GAA 1885-1985* (1985).

Louis Murphy – Luaí Ó Murchú

Louis Murphy was born in Newtownhamilton, County Armagh, on 30 May 1909. He was educated at Ballymoyer Primary School, St Mary's College, Dundalk, and the Salesian College, Pallaskenry.

He joined the Irish civil service in 1934 and, after appointments at Dundalk, Kilmallock, Bailieboro and Newcastle West, was in charge of the Social Welfare Centre at Listowel from 1946 until he retired in 1976.

He contributed short-stories and reviews to a wide range of newspapers and periodicals. These were in both Irish and English. Much of his writing in English was under the pen-name 'Redmond O'Hanlon'.

A life-long friend of Bryan MacMahon, he was a founder-member of Writers' Week, of which he was chairman from 1971 to 1977. His management skills were a vital ingredient in ensuring the success of the festival in its early years.

He published *St Killian's GAC, Whitecross: a History* (1996) and *Journey Home* (1997).

He died on 17 October 1999.

Chriss Nolan

Chriss Nolan was born in Lisselton on 25 December 1944.

She was educated at the local national school, St Joseph's, Mercy Convent School, Ballybunion, Mary Immaculate College of Education, Limerick, and University College, Dublin.

She was a member of the staff at St Joseph's Convent School, Dún Laoghaire, from 1965 to 1967, Tullamore National School, Ballydonoghue, from 1967 to 1968 and Lisselton National School from 1968 to 1975, when she was appointed a district inspector.

An occasional contributor to local historical journals, magazines and newspapers, she was a founder-member of The Friends of Maurice Walsh-Memorial Group. Members of this group also concerned themselves with the literary heritage of Robert Leslie (Bob) Boland and she edited

Thistles and Docks, the Poetry of Bob Boland in 1993. She has also been a founder-member of *The Ballydonoghue Magazine* and the North Kerry Literary Trust.

Pádraig Ó Conchubhair

Pádraig Ó Conchubhair was born in Ballylongford on 29 November 1946. He was educated at Lenamore national school, St Ita's College, Tarbert, and St Patrick's College, Drumcondra.

He was a member of the staff of Scoil Éanna, Ballymackney, County Monaghan, from 1966 to 1974 and since then has been teaching in Lenamore national school.

He has published *Scéal Scoile, Lenamore N.S. 1872-1992* (1992), *'Tá Sinn Ocrach' – Ballylongford and the Great Famine* (1997), *They Kept the Hills of Kerry – Kerry and the Rising of 1848* (1998), *Discreet and Steady Men – Kerry and the Rising of 1798* (1999), *'Leaba i Measc na Naomh' – Aghavellin Churchyard* (2000) and *A Visionary Enthusiast – Robert Emmett and his Kerry Connections* (2003).

John O'Flaherty

John O'Flaherty was born in Listowel on 21 November 1937. He was educated at the local national school, St Michael's college and University College, Galway. From 1959 to 2003 he was on the staff of St Michael's College. He has had a life-long interest in Listowel Races and published the comprehensive *Listowel Races – 1858-1991: a History* in 1992.

Pádraig Ó Loingsigh

Pádraig Ó Loingsigh was born in Kilgarvan, Ballylongford,

on 9 April 1934. He was educated at the local national school, St Brendan's Seminary, Killarney, Salesian Agricultural College, Pallaskenry, University College, Cork, Trinity College, Dublin, and University College, Dublin.

He served as a rural science instructor in County Galway from 1955 to 1962, in County Kerry from 1962 to 1966 and in County Cork from 1966 to 1974, and was a career guidance counsellor with Cork Vocational Education Committee from 1974 to 1992.

He edited *The Book of Cloyne* in 1977 and a second and revised edition in 1994. He published *The Ecology of Bogs* (1984), *Staigue Fort – Illustrated Guide* (1989), *Gobnait Ni Bhruadair* (1996) and *Bórdóinín: a History of the Parish of Cahirdaniel* (1999).

He died on 11 October 2000.

Mícheál Ó Murchú

Mícheál Ó Murchú was born in Mein, Knocknagoshel, on 22 January 1910. He was educated at the local national school, Blackrock College, St Brendan's Seminary, Killarney, St Patrick's College, Maynooth, and St Patrick's College, Drumcondra.

In 1932 and 1933 he taught in schools in Omagh and Castlecomer respectively. In 1933 he returned to Knocknagoshel and taught at Loughfouder national school from 1937 to 1947, when he was appointed principal of Knocknagoshel national school. He retired in 1975.

He published *Arise Knocknagoshel* in 1989, and *Memories of a Master* in 1977.

He died on 27 February 1999.

Nora Relihan, *née* Ryle

Nora Ryle was born in Abbeyfeale on 23 May 1929. She was educated at Killorglin national school, Presentation Convent, Milltown, County Kerry, and Presentation Convent, Hospital, County Limerick. A nurse by profession, she settled in Listowel in 1952 and three years later married Michael Relihan.

Her first love is the theatre, wherein she has featured as an actress, director and adjudicator. She was a co-founder of the Listowel Players in 1959 and Writers' Week in 1971 and the founder of St John's Theatre and Arts Centre in 1987.

She has worked as a freelance journalist and has contributed to radio and television programmes on RTÉ and Radio Kerry. One series for Radio Kerry was published as *Signposts to Kerry* in 2001.

PART III

Mairéad Carey

Mairéad Carey was born in Listowel on 14 July 1969. She was educated at the local Presentation Convent schools and the College of Commerce, Rathmines, Dublin.

She was a staff-member of the *Irish Press* from 1991 to 1995, *Ireland on Sunday* from 1997 to 2000, *Evening Herald* in 2000 and *Magill* from 2001 to 2003. In the periods between appointments she worked as a freelance journalist.

Mary Cummins

Mary Cummins was born in Castletownshend, County Cork, on 19 November 1944. She was educated at

Knocknagoshel national school from 1948 to 1952 and subsequently at the Mercy Convent primary and secondary schools in Ballybunion.

After a stint in the Department of Lands and later as a nurse, she joined *The Irish Times* in 1970. A collection of her 'About women' columns was published in 1996.

She died on 15 November 1999.

William Galvin

William Galvin was born in Listowel on 19 March 1970. He was educated at the local national school, Clongowes Wood College, Trinity College, Dublin, and King's Inns, Dublin.

He was a journalist with the *Irish Press* in 1993, *Irish Independent* from 1994 to 1996 and *Sunday Independent* from 1997 to 2000.

In 2000-2001 he worked for the aid agency Goal across Africa. Since 2001 he has practiced as a criminal law barrister.

Caitríona (Katie) Hannon

Katie Hannon was born in Listowel on 27 August 1968. She was educated at Duagh national school, Presentation Convent Secondary School and College of Commerce, Rathmines, Dublin.

A winner of the John Healy National Print Award in 2000, she was a member of the staff of RTÉ from 1988 to 1992, *Evening Herald* from 1992 to 1999 and *Irish Examiner* from 1999 to 2001. After completing the Journalistes En Europ work study programme (2001-2) in Paris, she joined *Ireland on Sunday* as political editor in 2002. She rejoined the staff of RTÉ in 2004.

Her *The Naked Politician* was published in 2004.

Conor Keane

Conor Keane was born in Listowel on 25 January 1960. He was educated at the local national school, St Michael's College and University College, Cork.

He was a member of the staff of the *Limerick Leader* from 1981 to 1988 and the *Kerryman* from 1988 to 1998. Irish property journalist of the year in 1997, he has been business correspondent of the *Irish Examiner* since 1998.

John (Seán) Keane

John (Seán) Keane was born in Listowel on 31 October 1961. He was educated at the local national school and St Michael's College and University College, Cork

He began his career as a journalist with *The Kingdom* in Killarney in 1985 and transferred to the *Kilkenny People* in 1988 where subsequently he also became a regional correspondent for *The Irish Times*.

Father Patrick (Pat) Moore

Pat Moore was born in Asdee on 10 June 1957. He was educated at the local national school, St Michael's College, St Brendan's Seminary, Killarney, St Patrick's College, Maynooth, and the Pontifical Gregorian University, Rome.

Ordained for the diocese of Kerry in 1982, since 1983 he has served in the parishes of Listowel, Rathmore and Lixnaw. For ten years he worked in adult and primary catechetics and was involved in compiling the *Alive-O* series for primary schools.

Fr Moore is a freelance journalist and a prolific contributor to local and national periodicals and is a frequent broadcaster on Radio Kerry.

Shane Phelan

Shane Phelan was born in Ballybunion on 25 December 1978. He was educated at the local national school, St Joseph's Secondary School, Ballybunion, and University College, Galway.

In 2000 he began his career as a journalist with the *Waterford News and Star*. From 2000 to 2003 he was on the staff of the *Evening Echo*. In 2003 he joined the *Irish Daily Star* and in the same year won the national Young Journalist of the Year award.

Joseph Stack

Joseph Stack was born in Listowel on 31 Mary 1968. He was educated at the local national school, St Michael's College and the University of Bournemouth, Dorset, England.

In 1992 he began his journalistic career with Radio Kerry. He worked as a freelance journalist from 1998 until 2003 when he joined RTÉ.

Noel Twomey

Noel Twomey was born in Listowel on 11 December 1970. He was educated at the local national school, St Michael's College, Dublin City University and University College, Galway.

He was a member of the staff of the *Kerryman* from 1993 to 1998, when he transferred to the *Irish Independent*.

Deirdre Walsh

Born in Ballybunion on 14 April 1968, Deirdre Walsh was educated at St Joseph's Convent primary school,

Ballybunion, Presentation Convent Secondary school, Listowel, and the College of Commerce, Rathmines.

She was a member of the staff of the *Corkman* from 1988 until she transferred to the *Kerryman* in 1991, where she was appointed news editor in 2000.

Jimmy Woulfe

Jimmy Woulfe was born in Listowel on 10 September 1952. He was educated at the local national school and St Michael's College.

He joined the staff of the *Limerick Leader* in 1971 and eventually served as news editor and deputy editor from 1981 to 2000, when he left to join the *Evening Echo*.

He published *Voices of Kerry* in 1994.[2]

---

2. For the biographical details above I am indebted to the persons described or, if they are deceased, from their close relatives.

VISUAL ARTS

The flowering of the visual arts in the area has been a feature of recent years. A number of factors have contributed to this. There is the growing self-confidence of people, a new emphasis on art in the schools and the art exhibitions organised in association with Writers' Week and latterly in St John's Theatre and Arts Centre. The success of Tony O'Callaghan and Olive Stack in both artistic and commercial terms has also been an inspiration to fellow artists.

Rebecca Carroll

Rebecca Carroll was born in Listowel on 13 May 1964. She was educated at the Presentation Convent Schools and the Limerick College of Art and Design.

She was a graphic designer in RTÉ from 1990 to 1998. Since then she has worked in her own studio at Littor Strand, Asdee. She has exhibited both within and without her native county and has completed a number of prestigious commissions.

Since 2000 she has organised exhibitions for the Brendan Kennelly Summer Festival in Ballylongford.

Finola Leane

Finola Leane was born in Listowel on 22 October 1922. She was educated at the Presentation Convent School and the Dominican Convent, Cabra, Dublin.

One of her teachers at Cabra, Sister Mary Ambrose, had a remarkable technique of flower painting on silk. This technique and her own love of colours are central to Finola's painting. Just as Listowel's writers have been influenced by the area's oral tradition she has found inspiration for her work in her memories of life in the town.

Her work is to be found in collections in Ireland, UK and the US. One of her exhibitions was presented by Joe Murphy in St John's Theatre and Arts Centre from 24 to 28 May 1995. It was an outstanding feature of the 26th anniversary of Writers' Week, of which she was exhibition director for graphics for many years.

Tony O'Callaghan

Tony O'Callaghan was born in Knockanure on 16 June 1940. He was educated at the local national school, De La Salle College, Waterford, and St Patrick's College, Drumcondra, Dublin.

He was a member of the staff of Sneem national school from 1959 to 1961, Moyvane national school from 1961 to 1970 and Scoileanna Réalta na Maidne, Listowel, from 1970 until he retired in 1998.

In the early 1970s, after working across a range of conventional artistic idioms, he developed a distinctive style and technique using copper as a medium. He exhibited his work in the Lartigue Little Theatre during Writers' Week in 1972, 1973 and 1974. The impact of these exhibitions was significant locally and nationally and led to an ongoing sequence of commissions from international corporations, public bodies, institutions and private collectors. Some of his works are to be seen in the Central Bank of Ireland and the Bank of Ireland, Dublin; the General Hospital, Tralee; Head Office, The Royal Society of Radiographers, London and Head Office, Irish Distillers Midleton. Heads of State, including five presidents of Ireland, have commissioned his work.

Much of O'Callaghan's artistic inspiration is prompted by the myths and legends of the Celts and from early Christian iconography. However, his later works have become increasingly abstract, such as *River Fort*, a sculpture sited in the Square, Listowel.

In 1993 his stature as an artist was recognised in a most successful retrospective exhibition in St John's Theatre and Arts Centre

He has been remarkably civic-minded. Apart from serving on local and statutory committees, including Kerry Vocational Education Committee, he was a Fianna Fáil member of Listowel Urban District Council from 1979 to 1998, during which time he acted as chairman for two periods.

Vincent L. O'Connor

Vincent L. O'Connor was born in Listowel in 1888. He was educated at the local national school, St Michael's College and the College of Art, Dublin. He was a member of the staff of Tralee CBS from 1907 to 1914. After emigrating to the US he was an associate professor of art at the University of Notre Dame from 1914 to 1958. Thereafter he worked in his own studio in Chicago. He was conferred with honorary life membership of the Palette and Chisel Academy of Fine Art in Chicago in 1972.

Olive Stack

Olive Stack was born in Duagh on 6 December 1974. She was educated at the local national school, Presentation Secondary School, Listowel, and Limerick College of Art and Design.

Listowel and its streetscapes inspired much of her early work. In 1996 she completed her first major commission: a mural for the office of Pierse and Fitzgibbon in Market Street, entitled *Lá an Aonaigh*. Other commissions followed from the Bank of Ireland, Listowel, the Church Street Development Group and for a mural dedicated to the life of playwright George Fitzmaurice. Between 1996 and 1999 she was commissioned by Table (Towards a better Listowel everybody) to produce paintings which were presented to the winners of the annual shop fronts competition, the aim of which was to encourage local business people to maintain their premises to the highest standards. These watercolour paintings featured the winning shop front in fine detail.

In September 1999 one of her paintings was presented to Moyvane-born Tommy Stack at a function to mark his achievements. It portrayed the jockey on 'Red Rum', the horse on which he won the Aintree Grand National in 1977. Another painting was presented to Killarney-born Jim Culloty. This captures the jockey on 'Bindaree' as they jump Beecher's Brook on their way to victory in the Grand National of 2002.

In December 1998 Olive Stack opened a gallery and studio at 4 Main Street. Here there is an ongoing exhibition of her work, together with limited-edition prints of her paintings. In recent years the subject matter of her paintings has become much more diverse, verging from seascapes and landscapes to figurative work.

Her paintings have been exhibited in Ireland, England

and the US and are represented in public and private collections in Ireland, England, US, Malaysia and Saudi Arabia.

Blue Umbrella Gallery

The Blue Umbrella Gallery is at 21 Church Street. With the help of North Kerry Together, it was set up by Mary Allen, Maura Mangan and Michelle O'Donnell and formally opened in October 2003. The stated purpose of this remarkable art gallery is to provide a place where local artists and craft workers can exhibit, explore and develop their talents. It has organised various art and craft activities to ensure greater awareness of and access to the arts by the community. Run as a co-operative, its members are: Chairperson: artist Michelle O'Donnell, Treasurer: artist Mary Allen, iron and stone sculptors Julie and Seán Finucane, ceramic artist Máire Mangan, artist Tricia Healy, photographer Sinéad Egan, calligrapher Caroline Collins, sculptor James O'Connor, and furniture designer Pat Lawless.[1]

---

1. Biographical details from the living artists listed. Information also from Joseph Murphy and Michelle O'Donnell. For the account of Vincent L. O'Connor, see *Irish Independent,* 24 May 1974. Sculptor Deirdre Gillespie, artist Karen Sugrue and weaver-tapestry artist Jacinta Scully Usher are also associates of the Blue Umbrella Gallery.

CULTURAL AND
TOURISM ACTIVITIES

During the past thirty years a remarkable number of cultural and tourism initiatives have flourished in this area.

Comhaltas Ceoltóirí Éireann: Listowel Branch

Comhaltas Ceoltóirí Éireann was established in Dublin in 1951. Its development since then has been remarkable. In 2002 it had 35,000 members in 400 branches. The bulk of these branches was in the 32 counties of Ireland but the organisation also has branches in Britain, US, Canada, Australia, Japan, Hungary, Sweden, Sardinia and Italy.

The primary aims of the organisation are: (1) to promote all kinds of Irish traditional music and dancing and (2) to foster the Irish language. To further these aims it organises each August Fleadh Cheoil na hÉireann at a provincial venue. Since 1972 , at the beginning of this week-long event a Scoil Éigse is held. At this summer school there are classes on the fiddle, concert flute, whistle, two-row accordion, concertina, píob oileann, harp, banjo, piano-accordion, traditional singing in Irish and English, set dancing, traditional dancing, accompaniment and the Irish language. From the earliest years of the Fleadh the final stages of national competitions have been held during the week. These are in four age-groups and cover the entire range of Irish traditional music and dance. The winners of each category begin their quest for honours in the spring at county level and progress through the provincial level to the finals at the Fleadh Cheoil. Over the years Fleadh Cheoil na hÉireann, the flagship event of Comhaltas Ceoltóirí Éireann, has enjoyed huge popular support and is now regarded as one of the major events in Ireland's cultural calendar.

The Listowel branch of Comhaltas Ceoltóirí Éireann was established in 1965 by Tim Brosnan, Mick Burke, Michael Dowling, Jerry Keane, Maurice Kennelly, Jack Larkin, Tim Leahy, Bernie and Marjorie Long, and Mick Regan. Under its stiúrthóir, Michael Dowling, it has been one of the organisation's most vibrant branches. Apart from organising occasional céilí, it has presented a weekly Seisiún: a mix of traditional Irish music, song, dance and storytelling each July and August at St John's Theatre and Arts Centre from 1993 to 2001 and subsequently at the Seanchaí Centre. However its main claim to fame has been its successful hosting of Fleadh Cheoil na hÉireann on as many as fourteen occasions between 1970 and 2002. The magnitude of this achievement can be gathered from the fact that during the week of the Fleadh Cheoil in Listowel in 2002, some 800 students attended the Scoil Éigse, 4,000 musicians took part in competitions and recitals, 6,000 more arrived for no other reason than to play in spontaneous sessions and it was estimated that 220,000 people visited the town.

---

1. Comhaltas Ceoltóirí Éireann, *The Living Tradition* (2003) *passim*, Comhaltas Ceoltóirí Éireann, *Treoir* (2003) *passim* and information from Michael Dowling.

Lartigue Monorail Museum

The unique Lartigue Monorailway was opened in 1888 to connect Listowel and Ballybunion. It ceased to run in 1924, owing mainly to substantial damage caused to it during the Civil War of 1922-3. Soon afterwards the company became bankrupt and went into liquidation. Preliminary steps were taken by the Listowel Monorailway Committee in 2000 to set up the museum. Within three years a replica engine, operated by diesel rather than steam, and two carriages have been constructed. Five hundred metres of track, complete with turntables, had been laid at the site of the former station of the Great Southern Railway. Plans disclosed by the Listowel committee in 2003 envisaged the completion of their project with the transformation of the derelict storehouse of the former Great Southern Railway into a museum, café and gift shop.[2]

Lartigue Theatre and Lartigue Theatre Company

The origins of the Lartigue Theatre can be traced to the spring of 1971 when local building contractor, Danny Hannon, conceived the idea of converting a stable behind the present Seanchaí Centre in the Square into a small theatre. Within a year with the help of other voluntary workers and a grant from the Arts Council the stable was transformed into a 50-seat theatre. A novel feature of the theatre was the absence of wing-space, and performers had to enter the stage by climbing down two ladders from the overhead dressing-room, in full view of the audience. During the next ten years a drama group, associated with the little theatre and known as the Lartigue Theatre

---

2. Information from Michael Guerin and Jack McKenna.

Company, presented plays by Moliere, Pinter, Chekhov, Fry, Priestly and Strindberg, in addition to the work of some of Ireland's best-known playwrights.

In 1982 the little theatre was no longer available and the Company was dormant for almost the next ten years. When St John's church was transformed into an Arts and Theatre Centre in 1991 the Company re-grouped and it has presented plays there ever since. The Company has also taken plays to Cork, Dublin, Tralee, London and several locations in the US. Danny Hannan, who was the director of the Lartigue Theatre Company from its beginning, was succeeded by Denis O'Mahony in 2002.[3]

Listowel Drama Group

During the past thirty years the Group continued its proud tradition of presenting plays practically every year as follows: Bryan MacMahon's *The Bugle in the Blood* (1974), Tom Coffey's *Anyone Could Rob a Bank* (1975), Dion Boucicault's *The Shaughraun* (1976), Oscar Wilde's *The Importance of Being Earnest* (1976), George Fitzmaurice's *The Magic Glasses* (1977), Thornton Wilder's *Our Town* (1978), Frank Moriarty's *The Couple Beggar* (1979), J.M. Synge's *The Playboy of the Western World* (1980), Bernard Farrell's *I Do not Like Thee Dr Fell* (1981), Philip King's *See How They Run* (1982), John B. Keane's *The Field* (1983), Brendan Behan's *The Hostage* (1984), Bernard Farrell's *Canaries* (1985), Ira Levin's *Deathtrap* (1988), Philip King and Falkland Cary's *Big Bad Mouse* (1989), Bryan MacMahon's *The Death of Biddy Early* and *Jack Furey* (1990), George Fitzmaurice's *The Magic Glasses* (1991), John B. Keane's *The Spraying of John O'Dorey* (1991), Bryan MacMahon's *The Time of the*

---

3. Information from Daniel (Danny) Hannon.

Whitethorn (1991), Thornton Wilder's *Our Town* (1992), Bryan MacMahon's *The Master* (1993), Brian Friel's *Dancing at Lughnasa* (1994), Bryan MacMahon's *The Honey Spike* (2000), Bernard Farrell's *I Do not Like Thee Dr Fell* (2001), Bryan MacMahon's *The Bugle in the Blood* (2002) and Marc Camoletti's *Don't Dress for dinner* (2003).

The Group had its greatest success in 1993 with the production of Bryan MacMahon's *The Master*. It played for fourteen nights at St John's Theatre and Arts Centre in Listowel and for another two nights in Siamsa Tíre's Stone Circle Theatre in Tralee.

The most versatile members of the Group were Bill Kearney, Brendan Landy, Marjorie Long, Anthony McAuliffe, Frank McInerney, Owen McMahon, Barney O'Reilly, Madeline O'Sullivan and Michael Whelan. As well as acting in plays they also directed and produced them.[4]

Listowel Players

During the first twelve years of their existence the Listowel Players staged a play practically each year. From 1972 onwards they continued to be prolific with the following productions: Robert Bolt's *The Flowering Cherry* (1972), Willis Hall's *The Long and the Short and the Tall* (1973), John B. Keane's *Sive* (1974), Brian Friel's *Philadelphia Here I Come* and Kevin Laffin's *It's a Two Foot-six Inches Above the Ground World* (1977), Hugh Leonard's *Da* (1976), P.J. Coen's *The Mountain is Gone* (1977), Barry Connors' *The Patsy* (1978), John B. Keane's *The Buds of Ballybunion* (1979), John B. Keane's *The Chastitute* (1982), John B. Keane's *Many Young Men of Twenty* (1982), Mrs Harry Wood's *East Lynne* (1983),

---

4. Information from Madeleine O'Sullivan.

John B. Keane's *Moll* (1984), Brian Friel's *The Communication Cord* (1985), Sigerson Clifford's *Nano* (1986), John B. Keane's *Sharon's Grave* (1988), Seán O'Casey's *The Plough and the Stars* (1989), G.A. Kennedy's *Job Crisis* (1990), John B. Keane's *Big Maggie* (1991), Tom Coffey's *Them* (1992), Tom Coffey's *Anyone Could Rob a Bank* (1994), Oscar Wilde's *The Importance of Being Earnest* (1995), Tom Murphy's *A Crucial Week in the Life of a Grocer's Assistant* (1996), Peter Schaffer's *Black Comedy* (1997), John B. Keane's *The Buds of Ballybunion* (1998), Dylan Thomas' *Return Journey* (1998), Bernard Farrell's *Happy Birthday, Dear Alice* (1999 and 2000), and Martin McDonagh's *A Skull in Connemara* (2001).

In 1988 with *Sharon's Grave* the group broke new ground. On the invitation of the London Irish Commission for Culture and Education and with sponsorship from the cultural affairs committee of the Department of Foreign Affairs and generous home-town support, they took the play on a London tour from 13 to 19 March. They staged performances at St Vincent's church hall in Dartford; The College, Ealing; Irish Centre Harringay; The Tramshed, Woolwich; and Anson Hall, Cricklewood. In 1998 the group was on the road again with *The Return Journey*. This time they played the Irish drama festival circuit and appeared at Cork, Tipperary, Shannon, Limerick and Kilmallock.

The Listowel Players had John B. Keane as their patron and Nora Relihan continues as their president. Pat Enright, Joe Murphy and Gertie O'Keeffe, but mainly Nora Relihan, directed and produced the plays presented by the group.

Apart from acting and directing, Gertie O'Keeffe has served at different times as secretary, chairman and PRO of the group.[5]

---

5. Information from Gertie O'Keeffe.

Listowel Singers

This choral group was formed in October 1980, with Colm O'Brien as director. Noreen Buckley became secretary when she joined a year later. O'Brien was born in Kilgarvan on 2 January 1933. He was educated Colaiste Mhuire, CBS, Parnell Square, Dublin, and University College, Dublin. Although he qualified in engineering, he went on to become a distinguished concert pianist. Under his aegis the aim of the Listowel Singers was twofold: to enjoy coming together to sing and to sing to the best possible standard. With an average active membership of over thirty, the choir divided into four sections: soprano, alto, tenor and bass. From the outset the group was determined to have a broad repertoire of music and eventually this extended to include Irish, classical, sacred, folk, popular and traditional music from many countries.

From its first year onwards the choir has been part of the formal opening of Writers' Week. It has performed in cabaret and concert at home and at venues in Europe and the US. Three time winners of awards at the prestigious Cork Choral Festival, it has won trophies at other festivals and has broadcast on RTÉ. To date the highlights of the group's overseas tours have been a visit to Rome in 1989 to sing High Mass in St Peter's Basilica and to perform concerts in the eternal city and a visit to New York in 1991 to take part in the 'I am of Ireland' concert in St Patrick's cathedral and in the parade on St Patrick's Day.[6]

North Kerry Literary Trust

In 1991 on the initiative of Deputy Jimmy Deenihan the

6. C. O'Brien, 'The Listowel Singers', *An Ríocht* (1999) pp.59-60.

North Kerry Literary Trust was established. Two years later it was responsible for the production of the *Rivers of Words* series – five 30-minute video documentaries based on the lives of Maurice Walsh, John B. Keane, Bryan MacMahon, George Fitzmaurice and Brendan Kennelly. With Pádraig de Brún as editor, it issued a reprint of D.C. Hennessy's *The Lays of North Kerry, and Other Poems and Sketches* (1872) in 2001 and Edward Judge's *The Collected Poems and Verses of Maurice Walsh* in 2003.

St John's Theatre and Arts Centre

The Theatre and Arts Centre in the refurbished church opened its doors in 1990. Under its manager, Joseph Murphy, it presents an ambitious annual programme. This includes theatre presentations by local and visiting groups, music, dance, exhibitions and film. The Centre's Arts Education Programme promotes contemporary dance, theatre and traditional Irish music and dance. It also organises summer schools each year for both primary and post-primary pupils.[7]

Seanchaí – Kerry Literary and Cultural Centre

Seanchaí, the Kerry Literary and Cultural Centre was formally opened in September 2000. It is housed in a refurbished nineteenth-century Georgian residence and modern auditorium. It has a performance centre, reading room, restaurant and gift-shop. Its Kerry Writers' Museum features George Fitzmaurice, John B. Keane, Brendan Kennelly, Bryan MacMahon and Maurice Walsh. In a room dedicated to the Seanchaí the tradition of storytelling is

---

7. Information from Joseph (Joe) Murphy. See also N. Relihan, 'St John's Heritage Centre, Listowel,' *Kerry Magazine* (1992-3) pp.16-18.

traced and Eamon Kelly acts as host, claiming: 'Storytelling is the oldest form of entertainment. In ancient Ireland the Seanchaí was held in such high regard that he sat at the table with the king himself'. A 'Writers' Week room' presents the history of Listowel's literary festival since its inception in 1971. The 'Landscape room' has an audio-visual presentation of the highlights of the scenery of North Kerry. The Centre fosters the rich musical tradition of the area, by promoting each summer a series of 'Seisiún': a mix of Irish music, song, dance and storytelling by local Comhaltas Ceoltóirí Éireann musicians. An archive of books and work by Kerry writers was begun in 2003. Cara Trant, the manager of the Centre, organises seasonal arts programmes each year.[8]

Siamsa Tíre: Ireland's National Folk Theatre

Fr Patrick Ahern, the genius behind Siamsa Tíre, was born in Moyvane on 5 March 1932. Educated at the local national school, St Michael's College, Listowel, St Brendan's Seminary, Killarney, and St Patrick's College, Maynooth, he was ordained on 23 June 1957. He has held a number of appointments in the diocese of Kerry and was administrator of Knocknagoshel parish from 1985 to 1990. From 1968 to 1973 he was in charge of the radio section of the Communications Centre, Dublin.

Fr Ahern's first appointment was to St John's parish in Tralee, where he was director of the church choir. In the early 1960s he gathered round him a group of the youngest members of the choir, who shared his enthusiasm for Irish traditional dance, music and song. Together they presented shows at the Catholic Young Men's Society (CYMS) hall.

---

8. Information from Cara Trant.

Initially they based these musical entertainments on the various activities on a farm in the past: butter-making, milking cows, feeding fowl, the threshing of corn with a flail, the sharpening of a scythe, or twisting a súgán rope. In preparing the shows Fr Ahern experimented with different choral arrangements and original choreography, and members of the cast used Irish traditional musical instruments, such as the bodhrán, the Irish harp and the uilleann pipes.

In 1966 the group, as 'Siamsóirí na Ríochta', presented a series of programmes on RTÉ. Two years later, at the request of the Tralee Tourist Office, they presented a show which they called 'Siamsa' (literally entertainment) during the summer holiday period. Both locals and visitors enthused about it. This led to an invitation in 1970 to play 'Siamsa' at the Peacock Theatre in Dublin. Demand was so great that the show was transferred to the Abbey Theatre where the group performed to full houses and excellent reviews.

In 1972, at the prompting of Brendan O'Regan, chairman of Bord Fáilte, and Eamon Casey, Bishop of Kerry, Ahern with the assistance of Patrick O'Sullivan, an architect, published a *Plan for Fostering Irish Folk Culture.* This envisaged: (a) the setting up of rural training centres in selected areas of the South-West region; (b) a training programme for these centres; (c) the provision of a new theatre in Tralee to be the 'shop-window' for the work of the centres; and (d) the setting up of a full-time performing company. By the following year Bord Fáilte had backed the plan with a grant of £50,000. In 1974 Siamsa Tíre, Ireland's National Folk Theatre, was established with Séamus Wilmot as chairman of the board of directors, Christopher Fitz-Simon, company secretary, Martin Whelan as manager and Fr Ahern as artistic director.

The first 'Teach Siamsa' was built at Finuge in 1974. A batch of young trainees was recruited and systematic training began. Another 'Teach Siamsa' was built at Carraig in Gaeltacht Chorca Dhuibhne, north of Ballyferriter, in 1975. Designed along the lines of the traditional thatched cottage, they had large kitchens with open hearths and there children were taught traditional dancing and music and to create their own mime and music presentations. It was also envisaged that each 'Teach Siamsa' would collect local folk customs for inclusion in stage productions. Over the years Fr Ahern and his colleagues have extended their repertoire and at different shows can have as their central themes: a May day celebration rooted in pagan times, the thatching of a house, a joyous harvest dance, or a sad love song.

In 1976 the company toured seven major cities in the US and performed for a week in the Palace Theatre, Broadway, to critical acclaim. During the following fifteen years Siamsa Tíre brought Ireland's Folk Theatre to many centres in Australia, Europe and North America. Some of these tours were particularly memorable. In 1980 the company represented Ireland at the International Indigenous Theatre Festival in Toronto and in the same year attracted 2,800 people to the Wembley Conference Centre, London, during the Sense of Ireland Festival. Siamsa Tíre performed for the Pope at Castel Gandolfo in 1981 at his first public appearance following the attempt to assassinate him. The company presented a special performance at the Rijksmuseum, Amsterdam, at a formal reception for the Dutch royal family in 1986. As part of the Bicentennial Celebration Siamsa Tíre performed at ten venues in Australia in 1988. The company represented Ireland again at Expo 1992 in Seville.

In the meantime, in 1977, the company had purchased and refurbished the Theatre Royal Cinema in Tralee. Here

Siamsa Tíre was based from 1978 until the official opening of its splendidly equipped Stone Circle Theatre in 1991. The imaginative design of this theatre was inspired by the ancient ring-fort at Staigue in south Kerry and proclaimed Siamsa Tíre's determination to cherish the country's cultural heritage from the earliest times. At the 'Stone Circle' the company, with seven full-time and many part-time performers, present a five-month summer season of folk theatre. And the theatre has become an important regional centre for the visual as well as the performing arts.

In 1995 Caimin Collins became associate artistic director and Ciarán Walsh was appointed director of the visual arts.

Apart from performing in Tralee the company continued to bring folk theatre to audiences at home and abroad, with a new emphasis on presenting it to schools and colleges. In 1995 third level students began a three-year course in Folk Theatre studies, jointly run by Siamsa Tíre and Tralee Regional Technical College. This became a four-year degree course in 2000. After the death of Martin Whelan in 2002 Morganne Kennedy was appointed manager.

In 1998 Fr Ahern stood down from his post as artistic director. An American theatre director, John Sheehan, filled the post until, in 2000, Oliver Hurley, a founding member of the professional company, was appointed the new artistic director. Under his guidance the company continued to expand its repertoire, adding new ideas and nuances to the unique brand of folk theatre that Siamsa Tíre had become.[9]

---

9. P. Ahern, 'The Siamsa Tíre story in brief', *Kerry Magazine* (1991) pp.6-8 and information from Fr Patrick Ahern, artistic director, 1974-98.

Writers' Week

After the success of its sessions in 1971, 1972 and 1973, Writers' Week has been continued each year at the beginning of the summer. It opens on Wednesday night and closes on the following Sunday night.

Its general format gradually evolved. The basic ingredients are the workshops. These deal with the various categories of writing. They are directed by well-known practitioners in the short story, poetry, the novel, biography, in writing one- or three-act plays or in preparing scripts for radio and television. One requisite for admission to a workshop is the preparation of an appropriate piece which the participant can refine during the week with the assistance of the director and the other members of the workshop. Bryan MacMahon inaugurated this component of Writers' Week and conducted workshops on the short story during the early years of the festival. He had seen at first hand the organisation of such workshops in the US, not least in 1965 when he had been a visiting lecturer at one of the best-known of these, that of the State University of Iowa.

Four or five lectures are held during the week. In the early years the emphasis in these was on the locality or local writers but gradually the subject of the lectures was determined by those invited to deliver them or by what is topical. Plays are presented each evening by local or visiting groups. A historical and literary tour of some part of North Kerry is a constant feature of the festival. There are exhibitions of various kinds, a book fair and book launchings. As the main aim of the festival is to encourage new writers, there are literary competitions for both adults and children. Lá na nÓg, a special programme for children, has been organised from 1972 onwards.

Bryan MacMahon and John B. Keane contributed in a curiously complementary fashion to the success of Writers' Week. By the early 1970s Bryan was a well-known author, a frequent lecturer at cultural and literary events throughout the country and was occasionally featured in programmes on Radio Éireann. A man of considerable personal charm, he was very popular with his fellow townspeople and was important in ensuring local support for the festival. He was a consummate publicist and in that regard had few equals as an ambassador for Writers' Week and his home town.

By the early 1970s John B. Keane had already established himself as a playwright of distinction. Through his columns in assorted newspapers his wit and dry folksy humour was widely appreciated. He was popular with other writers and was able to persuade many of them to take part in Writers' Week. Regarded as controversial, he appeared frequently on the panels of radio and television shows, where he never failed to draw attention to his work, Writers' Week and his native town. He was also a member of, and untiring in his support of, the festival's organising committee. Ultimately it was the members of these organising committees who ensured the continuing success of Writers' Week. With the death of Bryan MacMahon and John B. Keane in 1998 and 2002 respectively the festival lost its two guiding lights. However, under the astute management of David Browne, chairman of the organising committee, the festival continues to flourish.[10]

---

10. *Listowel Writers' Week Programmes* 1971-2003 and J.A. Gaughan, *Recollections of a writer by accident* (Dublin 2002) pp.26-38. For an account of Nora Relihan's contribution to the beginning of Writers' Week, see N. Relihan, 'Writers' Week in Listowel – the beginning' *An Ríocht* (2003) pp.69-71.

RECREATIONAL PURSUITS

Annual Race Meeting and Harvest Festival

From 1974 onwards Listowel Races continued to flourish, with attendances rising practically every year. In 1977 the Race Company added an extra day's racing to make the fixture a five-day event. From 1992 there were six consecutive days' racing at the autumn meeting. In 1997 the Race Company rented land contiguous to the 'Island' to facilitate races at new distances. In 2001 an extra spring meeting of two days was added to Listowel's race calendar. This followed the holding of point-to-point races at that time of year in 1994, 1995 and 1996 which did not have sufficient support to warrant their continuation. In 2002 the autumn meeting was extended to seven days.

In 1987 a Listowel Races Supporters Club was formed, mainly on the initiative of John Molyneaux. Its main aim was to sponsor some races and ensure that adequate prize money was offered for the winners of the various races. The following year a Ladies' Day was added to the programme of the race-meeting.

In the meantime the development of the race-course facilities continued. In 1974 a weigh-room complex,

administration block and improved stabling were
completed. Then in 1980 a new and larger stand replaced
the existing one. It was named the 'Hannon Stand' in
memory of Moss Hannon, a former long-serving director
of the Race Company. In 1990 a bar for owners and
trainers, as well as further improvements in stabling, were
provided.

The race course property is owned by the O'Leary
family who for generations have been most co-operative
with and supportive of successive Race Committees in
ensuring the continuing success of Listowel Races. The most
significant achievement of the current Listowel Race
Company was the conclusion in 1986 of a satisfactory
agreement with the family for the continued use of the race
course.

The Harvest Festival was, as ever, an integral part of race
week. For a number of years, however, preparations for the
festival had been less than satisfactory. Thus in 1976
disparate groups formed an all-embracing Festival
Committee. This committee, under the leadership of Dr
Johnny Walsh and Maria O'Gorman, was both energetic
and imaginative in promoting the festival. The outstanding
feature of the festival continued to be the All-Ireland Wren
Boys' competition, which drew large crowds from all over
Munster and beyond. From its inception in 1957 John B.
Keane, as its MC, ensured the popularity and success of this
event. Michael Dowling and others took over this role from
1978 onwards. And, beginning in 1989, a Harvest Festival
Queen was chosen on the Sunday night of race-week.

In 1992 John O'Flaherty concluded his comprehensive
account of Listowel Races:

Up to very recently many Listowel people would have
gone to the wall during the long winter months were it

not for the money they had earned during race-week. There were few Listowel families who have not benefited from the event one way or another . . . The races were vital to the economic life of the town ... They were for over a hundred years our only industry ... Thousands of visitors and exiles made their holidays coincide with the race-meeting and it was this meeting of old friends in the cheerful, convivial, carnival atmosphere of Listowel that gave the meeting its particular charm and appeal.[1]

O'Flaherty did not exaggerate the economic importance of the races to Listowel. For years many of the forty or so public houses in the town conducted as much business during race week as they did during the rest of the year. Since the 1970s this dependence of business people on race week has gradually declined. It is just as well as since the 1990s most of those attending Listowel races simply visit the course and spend little, if any, time in the town.[2]

Gaelic Games

Gaelic football has been for over a century the chief sporting interest of the people of Listowel and its vicinity. A number of factors contributed to this end. Not least is the success of the county team in the All-Ireland football championship and the National Football League. There is also a recognition that Gaelic games are native pastimes developed about the same time that other field games were being

1. John O'Flaherty, *Listowel Races – 1858-1991, a History* (Listowel 1992) pp.312-13.
2. John O'Flaherty, *Listowel Races – 1858-1991, a History*, *passim* and information from Brendan Daly, secretary, Listowel Race Company.

organised elsewhere. And there is an awareness that the Gaelic Athletic Association, which administers these games, was an integral part of the culture which inspired the struggle for independence.

Every parish in the area has its own GAA club. The club in Listowel, known as the Listowel Emmets since 1956, has had varying success during the past thirty years. The wet and muddy quality of the sub-soil in the Sportsfield continued to frustrate attempts to develop it into an all-weather playing-pitch. Extensive work had been undertaken on it in 1957-9. When this did not prove to be satisfactory, remedial work was attempted in 1970-1. Drainage contractors had the field again to themselves in 1979-80. Less than twenty years later their efforts were seen to be as ineffective as those of their predecessors. With commendable persistence the club attempted to solve the seemingly intractable problem again in 2001-3.

Listowel Emmets celebrated its centenary in 1985. There was a banquet with the GAA's president, the chairman of the Munster Council and the chairman of the Kerry County Board in attendance. *Listowel and the GAA: 1885-1985* was published. This included a history of the club from 1885 to 1919 by Father Kieran O'Shea and of the period from 1920 to 1985 by Vincent Carmody. It also carried the story of the Sportsfield by John Molyneaux.

Earlier the club had organised another important event which coincided with the re-opening of the playing-pitch, complete with a new stand in 1981. It was the formal naming of the Sportsfield Páirc Mhic Shíthigh: Sheehy Memorial Park. This was an appropriate recognition of Frank Sheehy's contribution to Gaelic games at home and further afield. Born in Listowel on 17 November 1905, he was educated in the local national school, Rockwell College, St Patrick's College, Drumcondra, and University

College, Dublin. After teaching in St Patrick's national school, Drumcondra, and the Endowed Primary School, Oldcastle, County Meath, he was appointed principal of his *alma mater* in Listowel in 1947. A life-long enthusiastic supporter of all things Irish, he set about improving the organisation of the GAA in Listowel and in the county. He served as chairman of the Listowel GAA Club from 1948 to 1952, Kerry County Board from 1951 to 1961 and Munster Council from 1956 to 1959 when he was one of the Association's four vice-presidents. He retired from his post in Scoil Réalta na Maidne in 1961 and took up a teaching appointment in Nigeria, where he died on 4 November 1962.

Apart from the better organisation of clubs inspired by Frank Sheehy and others, the participation of St Michael's College in competitions from 1953 onwards led to a significant improvement in playing standards in the area. College teams, prepared by John Molyneaux and John O'Flaherty, had remarkable success. A measure of their influence can be gleaned from the fact that three captains of All-Ireland winning football teams: Jimmy Deenihan, Tim Kennelly and Páidí O'Shea: were members of teams trained by O'Flaherty.

Listowel and the GAA 1885-1985 lists the club's roll of honours. This includes competitions won, the dedicated few who in each generation ensured that the amateur Gaelic games continued to flourish locally and the Listowel winners of All-Ireland Championship, National League, Railway Cup and All Ireland Vocational School medals.[3]

---

3. *Clár-cuimhne 1898-1960, Páirc na h-Imeartha, Lios Tuathail* (ed. John Molyneaux, Tralee, 1960), *passim*; *Lios Tuathail: Páirc Mhic Shíthigh* (ed. John Molyneaux, Tralee, 1981), *passim*; *Listowel and the GAA 1885-1985* (jointly edited, Tralee, 1985), *passim*, Páidí Ó Sé, *Páidí* (Dublin 2001) p.217 and information from Vincent Carmody, John Hartnett and John Molyneaux.

Since 1985 Listowel Emmets' senior team won the North Kerry Championship in 1991, 1997 and 1998, and the North Kerry League in 1995, 1996 and 2001. The team won the Kerry County Intermediate Championship in 2002 and thereby qualified to contest the Kerry County Senior championship. The Junior team won the County Junior Championship in 1999; the under-21 team won the North Kerry Under-21 Championship in 1997, 1998 and 1999 and the minors won the North Kerry Championship in 1985, 1986, 1998 and 1999.

The club's under-age teams, promoted by an enthusiastic Bord na nÓg, were successful at all levels from under-12 to under-16.

Since 1985 members of the club won All-Ireland football medals as follows: Patrick Kelly (minor 1988), Jerome Stack and Stephen Stack (junior 1994), Noel Kennelly and Brian Scanlon (under-21, 1998).

Stephen Stack in 1986 and 1997 and Noel Kennelly in 2000 joined the club's other recent winners of All-Ireland senior football medals: Tony McAuliffe (1939), Gary McMahon (1959, 1962)[4] and Tim Kennelly (1975, 1978, 1979, 1980, 1981).

The officers of the club for 2003-4 were Chairman: Tom Walsh, Secretary John Hartnett, Treasurers: Seán Moriarty and John J. Buckley, PRO: Andrian Kirby. Those of Bord na nÓg were: Chairman: Billy McElligott and Secretary: Eamon O'Connor.

---

4. Patrick G. (Gary) McMahon, born 31 August 1937, eldest son of Bryan, had interests, apart from football. He composed ballads, poems and the music of two masses in Irish.

Rugby Football Club

Rugby followers in the town maintain with some justification that their club, founded in 1893, must be one of the first IRFU clubs in Ireland. John (Jack) Macaulay and T.F. Cronin were members of it as well as the committee which acquired the Sportsfield in 1898. Both were enthusiastic rugby players, Macauley winning an international cup as a forward. But elements of pro-British sentiment and class-consciousness associated with rugby did not contribute to its popularity locally. However from the 1940s to the 1960s occasional rugby matches were played in the Sportsfield, largely owing to the enthusiasm of Gerald McElligott, proprietor of the Arms Hotel.

In 1978 the club was re-established. As the club has no permanent ground, most matches are played on a pitch reserved for rugby in the Town Park. For the 2003-4 season the club had two junior teams and one senior team which competed in the West Munster League and Galway-Foley Cup. In the 2003-4 the officers of the club were: Chairman: Denis O Sullivan, Secretary: Maurice O'Sullivan and Treasurer: Gerard Leahy.[5]

Soccer

Listowel Celtic Football Club was established in May 1963. It was the second soccer club to be set up in the county; preceded only by Tralee Dynamos Football Club which traces its beginnings to 1961. Listowel Celtic played their games on a pitch reserved for soccer in the Town Park. However, owing to a lack of players and shortage of funds, it was disbanded on a few occasions.

---

5. Information from Gerard Leahy.

In 1976 the club was re-established and affiliated with the Football Association of Ireland. The officers were: Chairman: John McAuliffe, Secretary: Patrick Kennedy and Treasurer: Dominic Scanlon. In the late 1970s and early 1980s the club's senior teams were remarkably successful in the Kerry Cup, Munster Junior and FAI Area Cup and FAI Junior Cup. In the 1990s the club's success in competitions was repeated. The club's attention to under-age and ladies' teams was vindicated by success in various competitions throughout the 1980s and 1990s.

From 1980 onwards most of the club's home matches were played in a rented field. Eventually this prompted the club in 2003-4 to launch a fund-raising campaign to provide a fully-equipped home ground, complete with changing and club rooms, at Tanavalla on the outskirts of the town. The officers of the club for 2003-4 were: Chairman: Aidan O'Connor, Secretary: David O'Brien and Treasurer: Dominic Scanlon.[6]

Community Sports Centre

Mainly on the initiative of Susan McKenna, Listowel Community Council was inaugurated in 1978. The executive committee of the Council decided in 1980 to build a Community Centre. This was completed and formally opened by the Tánaiste, Dick Spring TD, in 1985. The Centre has facilities for all kinds of indoor sports, as well as changing areas and a meeting room. A fitness room with modern equipment and a classroom were added to the Centre in 2001. The Centre is operated by Listowel Community Centre Ltd.[7]

---

6. Information from Dominic Scanlon.
7. Information from Patsy O'Sullivan.

Golf-Course and Club

Michael F. Barrett developed a nine-hole golf course on his property at Feale View in 1993. A golf club was set up in 1997 with the following officers: Captain: Seán Walsh, President: Michael F. Barrett, Secretary: Patrick (Patsy) O'Sullivan and Treasurer: Riobárd Pierse. The club had over 100 members in 2003.[8]

BLÉ (Bord Lúthchleas na hÉireann)

Bord Lúthchleas na hÉireann was established in April 1967. The Listowel club was affiliated to it in the following July. It was one of the organisation's most active clubs during the past thirty years. A number of its athletes were remarkably successful in track and field. Among the best known were Jerry Kiernan in the marathon and Geraldine McCarthy over 800 and 1500 metres. The officers for 2003-4 were: Chairman: Martin McCarthy, Secretary: Liz Keane and Treasurer: Eamon Whelan.[9]

---

8. Ibid.
9. Information from John Bunyan. For more, see David Kissane, *Wings on their Feet: A Story of Kerry B.L.E. 1967-1998* (Tralee 1998) *passim*.

VICINITY

Ballybunion

Ballybunion is widely known for its golden strands and seascape. In recent years its golf-course has become another important feature of the place.

The local golf-club was founded in 1893, when its members began to play golf near the sandhills between the town and the Cashen estuary. With the advent of the Irish Men's Amateur Closed Championship in 1937, the club had Thomas Simpson, the leading British golf architect, lay out the course. The first clubhouse stood at the sixth hole. The second, erected in 1971, was sited at the eighteenth. This was replaced by a more spacious clubhouse in 1993.

An ancillary course, the Cashen Course, was formally opened in 1982. Preparations for its development began in 1965, when the club bought 180 acres to this end. Robert Trent-Jones supervised the laying-out of the course. A large-scale modern practice facility to serve both courses was opened in 2003.

From the 1970s onwards the course became very popular with local and visiting golfers. In 1970 Herbert Warren Wind, the distinguished American golf writer, listed Ballybunion among the world's top ten courses and described it as 'simply the finest seaside links in the world'.

In 1971 Tom Watson played over the course and became one of its most enthusiastic advocates. In 1985 a delegation from the club went on a promotional tour of the US and by 2003, of the club's 700 overseas life members, 500 were from the US.

In recent years many of the well-known golfers from the international circuit have been around the course. A number of celebrities, including President Bill Clinton, have played golf in Ballybunion. This last was marked by the erection in 1998 of Seán McCarthy's sculpture of the president in golf-mode at the entrance to the town.

The club has established a special relationship with the world famous clubs at Wentworth and Pine Valley. It hosted the prestigious Murphy's Irish Open in 2000 and the Amateur Home Internationals in 2003.

The officers of the club for 2004 were: Captain: Donal Liston, President: Basil Patterson, Secretary: Fintan Scannell, Treasurer: Joe Guerin and Secretary-Manager: Jim McKenna.

The Heritage Centre and Museum was opened in 1990. It has a presentation on the Mesolithic, Neolithic, bronze and iron ages in the area. The centre also features early Christian settlements and has displays on the Lartigue Monorail Railway and the 'Marconi Radio Station'. This last was one of the first major wireless stations in Europe using the Poulsen-Arc transmitter. It was built in 1911-12 and functioned until 1920.[1]

---

1. Information from John Molyneaux.

Ballydonoghue-Lisselton

Following the publication of Steve Matheson's *Maurice Walsh, Storyteller* in 1985 a group from the village visited places in Scotland referred to in Maurice Walsh's novels. In 1992 'The Friends of Maurice Walsh-Memorial Group' were set up. The group, which included the energetic Chriss Nolan, decided to erect a bronze bust of their native son at the crossroads in Lisselton. Eventually the bust by Séamus Murphy was cast by Jim Connolly and was formally unveiled in July 1995. The group also conducted a short-story competition in 1995, 1996, 1997 and 1998. The aim of the competition was to draw attention to the life and literary work of Maurice Walsh and to encourage short-story writers. The group also promoted the publication of Edward Judge's *The Collected Poems and Verses of Maurice Walsh* in 2003. In the meantime, in 1994 the group and others from the area had again visited places in Scotland associated with Maurice Walsh and established links with the Stirling Literary Society which also had a keen interest in Walsh's novels and their provenance.

Members of the group did not neglect Robert Leslie (Bob) Boland, another well-known creative writer from the area. They collected his published and unpublished poems and verses. These and a private compilation of his work made in 1953 they issued in the handsome volume *Thistles and Docks: the Poetry of Bob Boland* which was edited by Chriss Nolan and published in 1993.[2]

Ballylongford

Life in the village during the past thirty years was a mix of

---

2. Information from Chriss Nolan.

the old and the new. The local GAA club undertook a substantial development of their playing pitch. This was completed in 2001. Due in no small measure to the encouragement and shrewd advice of Johnny Walsh, a veteran of many of Kerry's football triumphs, and his son, Jackie, teams from the village won the North Kerry Senior Championship in 1970, 1971, 1974, 1975, 1986, 1993 and 2000. The officers of the club for 2003-4 were: Chairman: Alan Kennelly, Secretary: John McEnery, Treasurer: Michael O'Carroll and PRO: John J. Walsh.

The Ballylongford Enterprise Association was set up in 1968. It provided better access and facilities for visitors to Carrigafoyle Castle, it had a new fire station built and, in conjunction with Ballylongford Boat Club, it had a slipway and clubhouse erected at Saleen Pier. But most importantly the Association inspired two annual festivals.

An oyster festival was organised in 1994. Since then it has been held annually in September on the weekend prior to Listowel Races. The festival was held to celebrate the resumption of oyster growing in the area. This activity in Ballylongford Bay was recorded as early as the sixteenth century. However, early in the last century it was no longer a commercially viable enterprise. The O'Rahilly, who was killed in the Rising of 1916, was the last person to farm and export oysters from the Bay. In 1986 Michael Finucane and others formed the Carrigafoyle Co-op, which obtained licences from the ESB, who had responsibility for the local tidal waters of the Shannon estuary. Following extensive trials between 1988 and 1993, the oyster beds were fully developed and the Co-op had forty members, growing oysters east and west of Carraig Island.

The Brendan Kennelly Summer Festival was inaugurated in early August 2000. A local committee, with Tim Kennelly as chairman and Justine O'Shea as administrator, organised literary and other events across four days. Apart from Brendan and his brother Paddy, other well-known literary persons participated. Art workshops for children and adults were conducted and art exhibitions were held. A splendid booklet to promote the annual festival was prepared by Mary Kennelly.[3]

Finuge

The Teach Siamsa continued to promote traditional Irish music, dancing and singing.

There were other significant developments which indicated what a small, vibrant village community can achieve. The local GAA club formally opened a new playing pitch in 1980. It was named James O'Sullivan Park in memory of a member of the local team who died in a tragic accident. The Finuge club was also successful on the field of play, winning the North Kerry Championship in 1966, 1987, 1996 and 2001, and providing players such as Jimmy Deenihan, Eamon Breen and Eamon Fitzmaurice for the county senior team.

In 1991 a local committee inaugurated the Seán McCarthy Festival which is held annually in August. Séan was a well-known balladeer and the main aim of the festival is to encourage the continuation of the ballad tradition. In 1992 the committee erected a sculpture of Séan by Jim Connolly in the centre of the village.

Another local group, since 2000, has prepared the village for its participation in the annual Tidy Towns Competition. To this end, it restored the village's last thatched house which dates from about 1750.

---

3. Information from Michael Finucane, Noel Lynch, Michael O'Carroll and Justine O'Shea.

The new bridge, linking Killocrim and Finuge, was completed in 2001. It replaced one built in 1908. In a sad commentary on that time, nearly all the 40 or so local men employed in its building immediately afterwards emigrated to the US.[4]

Tarbert

Apart from the ESB power station, the outstanding feature of Tarbert today is its Comprehensive School. Situated west of the village, it was established in 1973 as an amalgamation of three existing schools, St Ita's in Tarbert, James Dore's in Glin and Glin Vocational School. It caters for pupils from the parishes of Loughill-Ballyhahill, Moyvane, Glin, Athea, Ballylongford and Tarbert.

The school is an autonomous unit governed and financed directly by the Department of Education and Science and under the direction of a board of management. This board is comprised of three members, each a nominee of the trustees: the department nominates a member of the inspectorate, the Vocational Education Committee nominates its chief executive officer and the Bishop of Kerry nominates a representative. For 2003-4 these were Niamh Murray, Barney O'Reilly and Canon James Linnane respectively. Thomas McKeon was principal from 1973 to 1994, Joseph O'Sullivan from 1994 to 2002. O'Sullivan was succeeded by Mary McGillicuddy, as principal, and Geraldine Moynihan, as vice-principal. The school is co-educational, non-denominational and aims at catering for all ranges of ability.

---

4. Information from Fr Pat Moore. Deputy Jimmy Deenihan was largely responsible for the Seán McCarthy Festival, as he has been for the Lartigue Monorail Museum and Seanchaí-Kerry Literary and Cultural Centre.

The school building was extended in 1985 and again in 1994 to provide extra technical rooms, science laboratories, computer facilities and a stage. From the outset it has had an active Parents' Association. The library is dedicated to Thomas McGreevy and has a collection of books donated by Kit Ahern, a former TD for North Kerry. Reflecting its situation on the Shannon Estuary, the school crest is a lighthouse over the motto *Mens sana in corpore sano* – A healthy mind in a healthy body.

When the school opened in September 1973 it had 280 pupils and a teaching staff of 18. For 2003-4 there were 640 pupils, 47 teachers and a large ancillary staff.[5]

---

5. Information from Mary McGillicuddy.

THE OTHER LISTOWEL

This town in the county of Perth, province of Ontario, Canada, was incorporated in 1874 and in 1998 the townships of Wallace and Elma were amalgamated with it to become the town of North Perth. In 2002 the North Perth Chamber of Commerce promoted the new town as follows:

> The town of North Perth, located in the northern reaches of Perth County, is a strong, vibrant community. Formerly consisting of the townships of Wallace and Elma and the town of Listowel, the new town combines the best of small urban and rural environments. Its proximity to the twin cities of Kitchener-Waterloo provides the added benefit of big-city luxuries within minutes. These surroundings are enhanced by a large number of progressive farming operations and stately homes within our three communities. The local school system includes two public elementary schools and a public secondary school in the Listowel ward, one public elementary and one private elementary school in the Wallace ward, as well as one public elementary school in the Elma ward. Two universities and a community college are close by in Kitchener-Waterloo. Most Christian denominations are

represented within the town or very close by.

Medical facilities include the 50-bed Listowel Memorial Hospital that provides 24-hour emergency medical treatment and ambulance service. Eleven resident general practitioners staff the local medical clinic. A modern, well-equipped volunteer fire department provides first-class fire protection to the area. Policing is provided by the Ontario Provincial Police, North Perth detachment.

The North Perth public library provides a full-service library facility to residents of the community. Day-care facilities provide a safe, educational experience for your children.

Three modern arenas, two public swimming pools, tennis courts, soccer pitches and baseball diamonds form a basis for an active and progressive recreation programme. The Listowel golf and country club is described as one of the finest 18-hole courses in south western Ontario, and is presently being extended.

The 300-plus businesses now located in North Perth find this environment an excellent source of reliable, skilled labourers and services which help to make them competitive in world markets. Serviced and unserviced industrial-zoned land is available and waiting for development.

The Chamber of Commerce added the town's data profile:

Population: 11,622

Area: 119,833 acres

Incorporation: Listowel, 1874; Elma, 1857;
                 Wallace, 1858; North Perth, 1998

Transportation:	Provincial highways and an excellent county highway network
Energy:	Electricity, natural gas
Petroleum and Propane:	Available from many sources
Water Supply:	Listowel Ward supplied from groundwater, through deep wells operated by town
Sewage Treatment:	New sewage treatment plant built in 1994 and re-rated in 1999
Government:	Mayor, Deputy Mayor, 8 Councillors elected every 3 years by the town ratepayers
Town Office:	330 Wallace Avenue N., Listowel, Ph: 519-291-2950 Fax: 519-291-5611
Newspaper:	*Listowel Banner* (Wednesday publication) Ph: 519-291-1660 *Independent Plus* (Friday publication) Ph: 519-291-1660 *K-W Record* (daily)
Education:	Avon Maitland District School Board of Education Huron-Perth Catholic District School Board

Emergencies: Dial 911

Police: Ontario Provincial Police, North
                       Perth Detachment

Health Care: Listowel Memorial Hospital,
                       medical clinic, dentists, optometrists,
                       chiropractors

Until 1967 few people in the older Listowel were aware of
the existence of its counterpart in Canada. In that year,
following an invitation by travel agent Michael Kennelly, 41
residents of Listowel, Canada, led by their mayor, Carl J.
Wicke, attended Listowel Races. They were given a civic
reception and Mayor Wicke planted a Canadian maple tree
in the town park. The group in various ethnic costumes
added much colour and interest to some of the events of the
race-week carnival. A few also paraded as Canadian
Mounted Police on the 'Island' race course.

Naming of the Town

The settlement which became the Canadian town was
originally named Mapleton in 1855 because of the maple
forests in the area. When, however, the residents requested
the establishment of a post office, they were informed that
there was a place already called Mapleton. A public meeting
was held in 1856 to agree on a new name. Mrs Robert
Woods, who was a native of Listowel, proposed that the
settlement be re-named after her home town and this was
agreed. This was not the end of the matter. It seems that
someone in the department of the postmaster-general in
Ottawa added an extra 'l' to the name. This prompted
another public meeting to discuss the name in 1865 at
which the following resolution was proposed:

Whereas the name of our village has been erroneously spelled, in that a superfluous letter has by some means been attached giving it thereby an entirely wrong pronunciation and not consistent with the name evidently intended to be applied to it, and whereas the better to make the name harmonise both in spelling and pronunciation with that applied to a town in Ireland and also with that of a certain earl of the same name, we the citizens assembled do hereby resolve that henceforth, we will in all our business correspondence spell and pronounce the name with one terminating 'l', instead of two as present, viz. Listowel – giving the emphasis on the second syllable and resolve that we will use all our influence to carry out the spirit of the above resolution. We also resolve that the publishers of the forthcoming paper [*The Listowel Banner*] be instructed to publish the above in their first paper and to have the head of their paper comply with the above resolution and that the postmaster receive instructions from the postmaster-general to spell the word 'Listowel' in accordance with the above resolution.

W. H. Hacking, a general storekeeper, was the first postmaster to implement the wishes of his fellow citizens. He was typical of the early settlers. Born in Leeds in England, he was the son of Reverend James Hacking, the first Congregational minister in Canada. In 1817, when just seven years old, his family emigrated to Canada and settled in York County, Ontario. He served as postmaster in Listowel from 1856 to 1902.

Few Similarities

Apart from the name, there are few similarities between the

two Listowels. While the Irish town has a history extending over many centuries, that of the Canadian town goes back just over 150 years. John Binning (1812-1899) was the first settler in the bush, where Listowel is now situated. A native of Somerset in England, he served in the army for 11 years. In 1852, after leaving the army, he set out with his family into the 'Queen's Bush'. Eventually they came to a deserted shack which they occupied. Its owner had moved on. Later Binning met him and purchased the shack and 200 acres on which the earlier pioneer had staked a claim.

From the mid-1850s the settlement, begun by Binning and others, developed into a sizeable village. In 1859 it had a population of 700. In 1866 Listowel, with about 800 residents, was separated from the townships of Elma and Wallace and formed into a separate municipality. By 1874 the population had risen to just over 2,000. This was the population required for a place to be incorporated as a town. The lieutenant-general of Ontario issued a proclamation elevating the village into a town and the first municipal elections were held in January 1875. The town continued to grow, registering 2,575 citizens in 1899 and 5,400 in 1992.

The early citizens of Listowel were of English and Scottish stock. They remained intensely loyal to the British empire. It was a loyalty to which they never failed to give practical expression, not least during the two world wars. They were Protestant in faith and erected Anglican, Baptist, Congregational, Evangelical, Evangelical Lutheran, Methodist and Presbyterian churches. In addition, in the twentieth century the citizens had the benefit of the Bethel Christian Reform, Calvary United, Mennonite, New Apostolic, Pentecostal and United Missionary churches, as well as the Family Bible Fellowship, Jehovah Witnesses and the Salvation Army. In the early years Catholics had to go elsewhere for their religious services. It has been recorded that a Fr Kilroy from Stratford celebrated the first Mass in Listowel in April 1878. In 1954 the Catholic community established the church of St Joseph and this was replaced with a new modern church in 1991 to serve a parish of 300 families.

The pioneering spirit continued over the various generations of Listowel people. This manifested itself in a remarkable civic pride, community spirit and industriousness. Over decades, beginning with those associated with agriculture and logging, successful commercial enterprises were established. By the early twentieth century the town's furniture, knitwear and pianos were being sold throughout Canada and beyond. The steady economic growth of the town was halted only during the depression years in North America, with 1935 remembered as the town's blackest year. The foundations for the town's later remarkable economic progress and expansion were laid after World War II.

The residents had a strong attachment to local government and civic institutions. Party loyalty at local, provincial and national level generally divided between Conservative/Tory and Liberal. Primary education was available from the earliest years, as was secondary education from 1873 onwards. Some of the early residents played cricket. However, from the end of the nineteenth century the main team sports played have been American football and the national game of ice-hockey. There has been a rich tradition of choral singing, associated with Listowel District Secondary School, which has produced choirs that have excelled at choral festivals at home and abroad.

The town celebrates two annual festivals: Listowel Agricultural Fair, which was first held in 1856; and Paddyfest, which began in 1978. The former is held in July, the latter in March. The Paddyfest is promoted as a celebration of Irish culture and heritage. Keeping a watching brief over events at home and abroad is *The Listowel Banner*. This weekly was first published in 1865 and has over the years successfully seen off a number of would-be competitors. As the new millennium begins, the new town can look forward to a bright future under the enlightened and farseeing leadership of the municipal council and the town's chamber of commerce.[1]

---

1. Information taken from J. Hall (ed.), *Centennial at Listowel* (Listowel 1975) *passim*, *Listowel homecoming: July 31-August 3, 1992* (Listowel 1992) *passim*, *Brochure of North Perth Chamber of Commerce 2002*, J. O'Flaherty, *Listowel Races 1858-1991: a History* (Listowel 1992) p.184 and C.T. Bamford, 'Street talk', *The Listowel Banner* 29 June 1967.

ADDENDA AND CORRIGENDA

TO

LISTOWEL AND ITS VICINITY

(second and revised edition, Cork, 1974)

The material in this chapter is not included in the index or list of sources.

p.2　The cover design is based on 'Bételgeuse' by Victor Vasarély. Hungarian-born French painter, sculptor and graphic artist, Vasarély, who was born on 9 April 1908, died on 15 March 1997. He was the precursor and master of Op Art, which was at the height of its popularity in the 1960s. For more, see *The Times* 17 March 1997.

p.17　The place is named Listewell in Map 32, dated 1685, which is exhibited at Mucross House, Killarney.

p.35　　　　　　*Listowel Parish Priests*
　　　Thomas Carmody 1750-77
　　　Denis O'Sullivan 1792-1802
　　　James Walsh 1802-10

p.36　　　　*Church of Ireland Vicars of Listowel*
　　　(Archdeacon) John Murdock Wallace 1952-82

p.66   1906

John Cook, *Handbook for Travellers in Ireland* (London 1906) p.498:

> Listowel (Lios Tuathail, the fort of Tuathail), a thriving country town, with a population of 3605, on the banks of the Feale, which is a noble salmon and trout stream, though rather late in the season. It has a Square, in the centre of which the church stands conspicuous, and there is little else to see save a couple of ivy-covered towers of the old castle ...

p.66 The *Kerryman* of 13 December 1913 carried an interesting progress report on the Listowel Electric Lighting Company.

> The undertaking had been started a year earlier by a number of local people, in conjunction with the Ampere-Electrical Company of Dublin. A limited company was formed to carry out the scheme in which the contractor took a large share of the capital, the remainder was subscribed locally by 90 shareholders.
>
> At the beginning there was considerable opposition to the scheme but by December 1913 there were 45 public street lamps in operation and 170 consumers.

p.74   *Lixnaw connection with James Joyce's ancestors*

About 1680 William Fitzmaurice, 20th Lord Kerry, brought to Lixnaw from Connemara a stone mason, named Seán Mór Seoighe (Big John Joyce), to act as a steward on his estate. Seán Mór was accompanied by his brother. They were soon involved in the extensive work being done around Lixnaw. After 1747, when the fortunes of the Lixnaw family and estate went into decline, the Joyce family was given land at Athlacca in County Limerick. There they remained until early in the nineteenth century when some members of the family moved over the Ballyhoura Hills to Fermoy (newly developed by John Anderson and where there was a military barracks). One of these Fermoy Joyces was the grandfather of John Stanislaus Joyce (father of James Joyce) whose father, John Augustine Joyce (b. 1827), moved to Cork city (see John Wyse Jackson and Peter Costello, *John Stanislaus Joyce: the voluminous life and genius of James Joyce's father*, London 1997, pp.6–17).

p.76   Footnote 4: Read Bingham for Bigham.

p.94   Footnote 60:
It seems that Father O'Sullivan's loyalty to the establishment was more than counterbalanced by his curate's active support for the Whiteboys (see C.S.O., S.C.P. 1821).

p.94   Footnote 64
Another account in tradition places the hanging of a Whiteboy from a horse's cart at Gunsboro Cross.

pp.102–11, 154–63

1880s

Press reports and official documents indicate how disturbed the district around Listowel was at this time.

Freeman's Journal 16 February 1882:

Captain R.A. Massy, R.M., held a special court at the Gunsborough, North Kerry, at which 38 persons of the rural class were charged with being parties of an unlawful assembly on 19 January near Ballybunion on the occasion of a 'Land League Hunt'. A. Morphy, crown solicitor, prosecuted. J.F. Windle, solicitor, Tarbert, defended. An immense crowd was gathered in and around the courthouse and a strong force of military and constabulary was present. Those who did not enter recognisances were conveyed four miles to Listowel under an escort of Royal Marines.

NLI, Ir 94108, p.43:

This is a list of persons arrested and detained under the Protection of Persons and Property Act 1881 ('Forester's Act'). The list included:
Barron, James; Listowel, intimidation against rent-collection, detention 11 March–27 May 1882.
Breen, Matthew; Listowel, accessory to arson, detention 10 March–30 April 1882.
Enright, William; Listowel, arson, detention 15 June 1881–5 January 1882.
Gentleman, Francis; Listowel, arson, detention 10 March–13 April 1882.

Freeman's Journal 13 March 1882:

Moonlighters attacked the home of a farmer, named O'Connell, at Brosna. He and his wife were wounded.

Dublin Gazette 13 July 1882:

Kerry and Limerick were included in a list of counties which were the subjects of proclamations under Sections 8, 11, 12 and 14 of the Prevention of Crime (Ireland) Act 1882.

Section 8: gave additional powers to deal with riots and other offences ('aggravated crime of violence').

Section 11: gave powers to impose a curfew.

Section 12: gave powers of arrest of strangers found under suspicious circumstances.

Section 14: gave powers of search for arms and illegal documents.

Freeman's Journal 22 July 1882:

An inquiry was held at Listowel into a disturbance caused at a recent meeting addressed by Tim Harrington, secretary of the National League. Harrington conducted his own defence and stated that the crowd was not given time to disperse when ordered to do so. The Bench[1] consisted of H. Considine,[2] R.M. (chairman) and T. Butler, R.M. Captain R.A. Massy, R.M., for Listowel district, was examined. The government case was presented by A. Morphy, crown solicitor, Tralee. George

---

1. The Bench would appear to be the Quarter Session Bench which had certain inquisitorial functions under the Crimes Acts.

2. Heffernan Considine was born at Pallas Green, County Limerick, in 1846. He was educated at Trinity College, Dublin. From 1882 to 1900 he was R.M. for the Tralee district. In 1900 he became deputy inspector general of the constabulary, the first Catholic to reach that position. He was knighted in 1908 and retired in 1911.

Bolton,[3] crown solicitor, Tipperary, appeared on behalf of the constabulary.

Freeman's Journal 21 April 1885:

During his visit to Ireland in 1885 the Prince of Wales visited Killarney. Herein are two reports of his return journey to the border of County Limerick. The first is a general report of the mixed reception given to the royal party, the second details of the very different reactions the royal visit provoked at Listowel.

1.

In all cases two parties were on the platform to greet the prince: loyalists with addresses of welcome and catch-crying nationalists whom the police attempted to keep as far out of sight as possible. At Killarney 'God save the Queen' was played by a

---

3. Bolton appeared in many cases in the West of Ireland at this time as 'special crown solicitor'. He was a most controversial figure and was mentioned in many of the grand debates in the House of Commons. He was expert at seeking out and using the informer. He refers to the above episode in an appeal submitted to the authorities at a time when his job was in danger due to his bankruptcy. In a letter, dated 3 June 1854, to the chief secretary, Bolton wrote from his office at 6 Ely Place.

In 1880-1 the promoters of agitation went deliberately to work to make the constabulary discontented and disloyal [this is a reference to a police strike in Limerick] and having failed next attempted to intimidate them by prosecuting them on every occasion upon which they had to resort to force for their own protection. This led to inquisitions at Ballyragget, Belmullet, Ballina and to prosecutions at Fresford and Listowel. I defended the constabulary in all these cases ...

military band. At Tralee a guard of honour drawn from the Yorkshire regiment and a military band was stationed close up, while crowds in the fields close to the station rushed along the railway line crying 'Up Parnell'.

At Listowel a few people cheered on the platform, where Mr George Sandes gave the princess a bouquet. On the railway bridge and in the fields nearby were the Parnellites and on the road by the station the nationalist band of the district played 'God save Ireland'. Nationalist banners displayed on the road had the following slogans: 'We'll have no Prince but Charlie', 'Remember Mallow', 'Remember Barrett and Poff', 'Remember Myles Joyce', 'Avoid Foxy Jack', and 'Down with Castle Rule'.

Before reaching Listowel the train passed by Lixnaw and Ennismore. At Lixnaw a crowd of people assembled on the walls near the station and stood silent with folded arms. At Ennismore a crowd of about 30 people, including the police, stood on the platform and pelted the royal train with primroses, while behind them in a field was a hostile crown chanting 'Up Parnell', in their midst a woman holding a black flag.

2.

At Listowel entry to the station was by ticket. Their royal highnesses, the Prince and Princess of Wales were accompanied by Prince Victor and suite. The platform was prettily decorated with flags and evergreens, under the supervision of Mr Isaac McMahon, builder, Listowel. On Saturday Mr

McMahon borrowed scaffolding poles for the occasion from Mr John Stack, C.T.C., Listowel. On subsequently hearing of the use they were being put to, Mr Stack and twenty patriotic youths marched to the station and forcibly removed the poles on Sunday evening.

A meeting of citizens held in the National League rooms protested against the address of welcome which was being presented on their behalf. The meeting was presided over by Mr Adam Fitzell.

Police in the charge of D.I. Reid (Killaloe) and D.I. Tyacke (Listowel) tried on a number of occasions to disperse the crowd and Mr George Sandes J.P., on a number of occasions ordered the band in the nearby field to disperse. One hundred and fifty people on the platform wore primroses in their buttonholes.

As the train left the station women waved black shawls and afterwards the band paraded the streets playing patriotic airs followed by 5,000 people singing 'God save Ireland' and 'The wearing of the green'. A meeting then assembled at Stack's Buildings presided over by J. Flavin who said that public opinion had done that day what George Sandes and his flunkies had endeavoured to prohibit. Mr W.A. Cronin followed and then Mr M. Murphy, both of whom received a very enthusiastic reception. Murphy said they had there today a mixed assembly: some who believed in agitation, while others believed that Ireland could only be regenerated by the sword (loud applause).

Freeman's Journal 22 November 1886:

> Two men, Timothy Scanlon and William O'Sullivan were arrested for firing on a police patrol at Ballylongford. They were brought up in custody before Captain R.A. Massy, R.M.

Irish Catholic 5 May 1888:

> Daniel Hayes and Daniel Moriarty were executed in Tralee jail for the murder of James Fitzmaurice at Lixnaw on January 31st. They were sentenced to death at Wicklow Assizes. The venue of the trial was changed from Kerry under the provisions of the Crimes Act. The crown exercised its right of challenge to every Catholic juror on the panel. It did likewise at all capital cases at that Assize. Mr Corbet is to raise the matter in the House of Commons.
>
> Also condemned at that Assize was Kirby for the Liscahane murder: he died protesting his innocence.

Richard Albert Massy

Richard Albert Massy was the resident magistrate for Listowel district during those years.

Dr Gerald McElligott, whose residence 'Mount Rivers' he subsequently rented, described him as 'the archetype of everything unpleasant in the administration of English law in Ireland'.

One gleans how Massy viewed himself from the following letter, dated 24 November 1888, which he wrote to Colonel Turner, Divisional Magistrate, Ennis.

Having been passed over by juniors on several occasions I have the honour to submit this my claim for promotion to the first class which is based upon the following grounds chiefly: Appointed R.M. on 10 September 1867 and have now nearly completed 21 years of active and faithful service during which time I have never been censured by the government but on several occasions have been commended for the manner in which I have discharged my magisterial duties ... I exerted myself impartially and energetically during the Land League times in the preservation of the peace to the risk of my own life when in charge of bodies of troops and constabulary acting in maintaining order in the presence of large and excited mobs, also at night frequently with patrols of military and constables for the prevention of crime and the detection of criminals and in imminent danger of assassination, and I was for a time obliged to be guarded by armed constabulary, the warning of an intended attempt on my life being conveyed to me from Dublin Castle.

I have been successful and instrumental in bringing offenders to justice in some serious Whiteboy offences such as the Lenahan outrage, Fealebridge outrage, Drumtrasna (Co Limerick) outrage ... also in the Islandanny murder [the murder of a mother by her demented son], the murder of James Fitzmaurice, for my action in which I was highly commended by the rt hon, the attorney general, and in numerous prosecutions under the Criminal Law Procedure Act, including the case against Timothy Dowling for intimidation ...

The Record of Service Book in the State Paper Office reads: 'Massy, Richard Albert (Capt); native, Tipperary, a Protestant, declared under CL & P Act 23 July 1887; aged 27 when appointed to Manorhamilton, first station, 1867; Listowel, March 1876 until his death 21 September 1889; served in 60th Royal Rifles, India, Canada, England and Ireland for seven years, and in New Zealand; promoted 1st class 3 July 1889.'

p.105 Footnote 110

Gerard O'Callaghan's father, Edmund, who was the great-grandfather of Maurice Gerald McElligott, was press-ganged into the navy. He served with Nelson. After the battle of Trafalgar in 1805, he retired to Listowel and with the prize money from his naval service built Leahy's Corner House at 1 The Square. According to tradition it was one of the earliest houses in the town with a slate roof (information from Bridie O'Donnell, née Leahy).

p.106   1891
                    Meeting of Parnell and Kitchener

The only recorded meeting of Parnell and Kitchener took place in Listowel on 13 September 1891. It was witnessed by Michael MacDonagh. A native of Limerick, he was one of the most distinguished journalists of his time. In 1991 he was a reporter on the *Freeman's Journal*. Seven years later he began his life-long connection with the London *Times*, reporting from the Press Gallery of the House of Commons.

   On the weekend 12-13 September Parnell was in Listowel to address a meeting (his third last) in support of his leadership. He spent the previous night at Kilmorna House as a guest of his close fried and supporter, Pierce O'Mahony, MP.

At that time the 41-year-old Kitchener was adjutant-general of the Anglo-Egyptian army. While on a brief visit to Dublin, he travelled down to North Kerry and Listowel to renew his acquaintance with the places where he had spent his early boyhood with his brothers.

MacDonagh was in Listowel to report on Parnell's meeting for his newspaper. In one of his favourite reminiscences he frequently recalled: 'As a *Freeman's Journal* reporter I was with Parnell and Mahony on the way to the Market Place [The Square] for the meeting. They met Kitchener who being known to Mahony was stopped by him and introduced to Parnell.'

Less than four weeks later Parnell was dead and twenty-five years later Kitchener was drowned at sea.[4]

p.132 Footnote 214

For an interesting reference to the Banshee, see Arabella Kenealy, *Memoirs of Edward Vaughan Kenealy, LL.D.* (London 1968) p.59.

p.189 For further sources on faction-fighting, see S. Breathnach, *The Irish Police from the Earliest Times to the Present Day* (Dublin 1974) and P.D. O'Donnell, *The Irish Faction Fighters of the Nineteenth Century* (Dublin 1975).

---

4. For this and Michael MacDonagh's fascinating comments on these two remarkable Irishmen, see *Irish Weekly Examiner* 1 March 1979.

p.190 Footnote 4

Read letter, for letter.

p.235 Footnote 116

For more, see B. Ó Cathaoir, 'Michael O'Mahony: Kerry scribe', *Iris Muintir Mhathghamhna* 10 (1980) 48-9.

p.245 Footnote 142

Read Catholic for Caholic.

p.251 Footnote 163

In recalling his school-days Edward Vaughan Kenealy (1819-80), member of the House of Commons and distinguished member of the English and Irish Bars, described one of his teachers named Casey as 'the most expert flogger in Cork city'. His school was in Brown Street and over a period of ten months Kenealy was flogged by Casey once and sometimes twice a day on his hand or naked back 'until the former grew horny and the latter became hardened like an alligator's'. Eventually Kenealy received such a beating that he had a fit of convulsions and was taken home insensible (Arabella Kenealy, *Memoirs of Edward Vaughan Kenealy, LL.D.* (London, 1908) pp.39-40.

p.268 Footnote 19

See also William Shortis, 'The Lartigue Railway', *Strand* 15 (Jan-June 1898) pp.956 and ff.

p.275 Last line

Read it.

p.297 Footnote 55

An interesting description of the thatched Ballinruddery House is to be found in the *Dublin Penny Journal* of 12 March 1836. About that time some of the Ballinruddery lands were sold to Lord Salisbury but they were bought back again by the FitzGeralds c. 1850 (information from Sir Adrian FitzGerald). An excellent unpublished article by John J. Molyneaux on Ballinruddery in general and the association of the knights of Kerry with it in particular is to be found in the Local History Archive, Kerry County Library, Tralee.

p.305 William Francis Hare died on 12 March 1997, aged 90. For a splendid obituary on this remarkable person, see *The Independent* 13 March 1997.

p.327 Coilbhee: Sir John Benn-Walsh was an absentee landlord who owned 8,900 acres in County Kerry and 2,200 acres in County Cork. These had been acquired by his great-uncle in 1764. Benn-Walsh was an exacting landlord and recorded his visits to supervise his lands. His journals, edited by James Donnelly, provide a fascinating account of his dealings with his tenants in the townland of Coilbhee, also known as Gortshanavoe, near Listowel (see *Cork Examiner* 23 January 1976).

p.340 After Captain Wilkinson's death the office of Ulster King of Arms was re-named that of the Chief Herald but the title was still used in the UK. Cf. De Bret 1975, p.2142.

p.346 Footnote 10

Manchester Martyrs' celebrations were held annually in Listowel under the aegis of the Urban District Council when D.J. Flavin served as its chairman (see *Kerry Sentinel* 15 November 1913).

p.350   *1916*

After the release of prisoners in 1917 Michael Collins wrote to John and Mary Mulvihill of Ardoughter, Ballyduff, informing them that their son Michael had been buried in Glasnevin Cemetery with other Irish Volunteers and members of the Irish Citizen Army. His name was among those subsequently inscribed on the monument at the burial plot. In 1966 Margaret Mulvihill, sister of Michael, wrote to Nicholas O'Neill, an ex-member of the Dublin Metropolitan Police and a native of Boherbawn, which is close to Ardoughter, asking him to confirm that he had seen Michael Mulvihill's body in the vicinity of the General Post Office in Dublin. O'Neill had moved to England, whence he wrote to Margaret on 5 May 1966 as follows:

I am in receipt of your letter of the 2nd inst. re death of your brother Michael during Easter week in Dublin. Yes, I saw the dead body of your brother Michael lying in Moore Lane off Henry Street and at the rear of O'Connell Street, Dublin, after the surrender; also, the dead body of The O'Rahilly lying in Henry Street close by. I had no further time for scrutiny as we were hurriedly taken into O'Connell Street to prevent looting.

What does it matter where he was shot? He lost his life fighting for his country's cause. Peace be to his dead soul.[5]

_____

5. Information from Austin Kennan.

p.361 *1918*

In May 1918 the Listowel company of the Irish Volunteers planned a raid on the RIC barracks to obtain arms and ammunition. They organised a riot at Moyvane which drew nearly all the policemen out of town. Several members of the company, including Edward Browne, Paddy Guerin and Paddy Landers, climbed the wall, which divided McKenna's timber-yard and the barracks, and took all the guns and ammunition they could lay their hands on. The ensuing investigation did not identify the culprits. However, some guns and ammunition were found in Jack McKenna's premises. One of the leading Sinn Feiners in the country at that time, he was accused of the illegal possession of these, sent to Cork to face a court-martial and sentenced to a year with hard labour in Belfast jail. He was released on Christmas Eve.

p.369 Footnote 87, last line

Read popular for popula.

p.432 *1914*

Read German spy for Germany spy. Carl Hans Lody was a German naval officer. He acted as a spy, was arrested by police in Ireland and after the outbreak of war in 1914 was executed in the Tower of London. For further details, cf. BBC 2 programme on MI5.

p.457 Footnote 2

Read Denis for Deiis.

p.477 Footnote 6

Monsignor John D. Horgan died on 8 July 1980. Reverend Dr Joseph Nolan was on the staff of St

Patrick's College, Maynooth, from 1971 to 1975. Reverend Dr Conor Martin died on 22 September 1980.

p.489 Mrs Mary Kathleen O'Sullivan died in 1981. Liam Shine, the 'Man on the bridge' columnist in the *Evening Herald*, died on 12 January 1981.

p.497 From the 1970s onwards the Southern Health Board became involved in the management of the District Hospital which continued to be under the supervision of the Sisters of Mercy. Between 1983 and 1985 the hospital was extended to include a modern unit of continuing care for thirty patients. It replaced St Joseph's, the former geriatric unit.

In 1988 the sisters vacated their convent, St Brigid's. It was taken over by the Southern Health Board, refurbished and thereafter, as 'Senan House', was a day-hospital under the aegis of the Kerry Mental Health Service.

In 1990 the five sisters, after residing for almost two years in the nearby Presentation Convent, moved into their new convent in Greenville. Five years later a remarkable tradition of service, which lasted for 112 years during which time one of the sisters was head-nurse or matron of Listowel's hospital, ended when Sr Mary O'Brien retired.

In 1977 the role of the District Hospital was re-defined, it was re-named Listowel Community Hospital and two of the Sisters of Mercy continued to be members of the nursing staff. In that year also two hospice rooms were opened, following fund-raising by a local hospice committee. In 2002 Writers' Grove House with fourteen beds was built by Kerry Mental

Health Service and in 2002 the Welfare Home, re-named Áras Mhuire, was upgraded to the status of a nursing home and continued to be managed by a local committee (information from Sr Margaret Flynn).

p.498 Donovan Hadley died on 30 December 2003.

p.543 Patrick B. Kirby of Listowel, brother of Frs Edward A., Thomas and Timothy Kirby, was professed as a Christian Brother c. 1885.

pp.544-9

Francis Buckley of Listowel was ordained c. 1890 for the diocese of Auckland. His brother, John, was ordained c. 1900 for the diocese of Sydney.

J.J. Cronin of Listowel was educated at St Patrick's College, Carlow, and ordained in 1909 for the diocese of Wichita.

Michael Kirby of Listowel was educated at St Patrick's College, Carlow, and ordained c.1897 for the diocese of Sydney.

T. Kirby of Listowel was educated at St Patrick's College, Maynooth, and ordained c. 1895 for the diocese of Kerry.

John Molyneux of Listowel was educated at Mundelein College, Chicago, and ordained in 1916 for the diocese of Des Moines.

Timothy Naughten of Listowel was educated at St Patrick's College, Thurles, and ordained in 1915 for the diocese of Oregon.

M. O'Connell of Listowel was ordained c. 1893 for the diocese of New York.

Joseph O'Connor of Listowel was educated at the Irish College, Paris, and ordained c. 1896 for Illinois.

His brother, Michael, was also educated at the Irish College, Paris, and was ordained c. 1900 for Illinois.

Richard Alphonsus O'Connor was born in Listowel on 13 January 1838. He arrived with his parents in Upper Canada in 1841. He was educated at St Michael's College, Toronto, and the Grand Seminary, Montreal. Ordained on 2 August 1861, he served in parishes in the diocese of Toronto from 1861 to 1889. He was appointed bishop of Peterborough in 1889 and died on 23 January 1913. For more on this remarkable missionary bishop, see Edgar J. Boland, *From the Pioneers to the Seventies: A History of the Diocese of Peterborough*, Peterborough 1976, pp.23-41.

Timothy Walsh of Coolaclarig, Listowel, was ordained in 1901 and was a member of the Franciscan Order from 1894 to 1919. For the following comprehensive profile I am indebted to his nephew, Martin Kennelly.

Timothy Walsh was born on 7 May 1878 in Coolaclarig, Listowel, County Kerry, the son of Thomas and Hanorah (Buckley).

Attended Clounmacon National School, 30 September 1885 – 15 November 1890. Probably attended St Michael's College. Records of those years were destroyed by fire.

He was received into the Franciscan Order on 8 August 1894 at Gorton, Manchester, England, and was given the religious name Jerome (Hieronymus). He made his temporary profession on 9 August 1895 at the junior seminary at Buckingham. His solemn profession was made on 4 May 1899 at the House of Studies, Forest Gate, London. He was ordained a priest 27 January 1901.

In 1903 he is mentioned among the community

at the friary in Gorton, Manchester, where he seems to have remained until 1906, when his name no longer appears. In 1908 he was appointed Guardian (superior) of the community in Gorton, Manchester. In 1910 he is no longer mentioned among the members of that community and there is a new Guardian. At the 1911 provincial chapter he received one vote for 'Definitor' (provincial councillor). In 1913 he was appointed as vicar of the friary at Stratford, London.

In May 1915, Father Jerome joined the British army and served, as a chaplain to the forces in France, until September 1919. He was shell shocked in combat.

After disembarkment in 1919, he successfully received secularisation from the Franciscan Order to serve with Bishop Garrigan in the diocese of Sioux City, Iowa. He arrived at the port of New York in December 1919. He served as a curate at St Jean Baptiste parish in 1920 and at St Joseph in 1920-23. He received a transfer to the diocese of Jefferson City, Missouri, where he served from 1924 to 1926 at Immaculate Conception and from 1927 to 1928 at the Shrine of St Patrick, St Patrick, Missouri.

On 8 June 1928 Father Jerome Walsh died in Keokuk, Iowa. He was buried in Calvary Cemetery, Chicago, Illinois.

p.549 Line 10 from bottom
Read James A for James
Des Moines for St Paul

Line 9 from bottom
Read 1913 for c. 1914
Des Moines for St Paul

p.575 Include Maher, S, *The Road to God Knows Where* (Dublin 1972).

p.578 Transpose line 6 from bottom of page to bottom of entry under Ó Lúing, S.

p.592 Read Banshee 133, 456 for Banshee 456.

p.605 Finuge 40, 44, 510.

p.615 Transfer top 8 lines on col 2 to the top of col 1.

p.618 Transfer bottom 7 lines on col 1 to the top of col 1.

p.629 Read Pearse, Patrick (1916) for Pearse (Patrick, 1916).

SOURCES CITED IN FOOTNOTES

A
UNPUBLISHED

Dublin, National Museum of Ireland, Kildare Street
　　98E 0293.
　　1A/127/83.
　　1A/3/77.
　　1975/256.

Limerick, IDA Ireland, Chandler House, Henry Street
　　Report on operations in Ireland of Neodata Services Inc., Boulder, Colorado.

Listowel, Presentation Convent
　　Diary.

B
PUBLISHED

Ahern, Patrick, 'The Siamsa Tíre story in brief', *Kerry Magazine* 1991.
Bamford, Cyril T., 'Street talk', *Listowel Banner* 29 June 1967.
Booklet (St Michael's College, Millennium Ball 17 December 1999).

Brochure of North Perth Chamber of Commerce 2002.

Cahill, Mary, 'The end of a mystery – how the gold "box" from Ballinclemesig was used', *Kerry Magazine* p.14 (2003).

Comhaltas Ceoltoirí Éireann, *The Living Tradition* (2003).

Comhaltas Ceoltoirí Éireann, *Treoir* (2003).

Dolley, Michael, 'A hoard of the so-called "gun-money" from Causeway', *Kerry Archaeological and Historical Society Journal* 7 (1974).

Facilities for industrialists – what Listowel has to offer (Listowel 1960).

Gaughan, J. Anthony, *Recollections of a Writer by Accident* (Dublin 2002).

Hall, Joanne (ed.), *Centennial at Listowel* (Listowel, Canada, 1975).

Healy, Patrick, 'Dugout wooden boat in the estuary of the Cashen', *Kerry Archaeological and Historical Society Journal* 14 (1981).

Healy, Patrick, 'Container of butter from a bog at Banemore', *Kerry Archaeological and Historical Society Journal* 14 (1981)

Irish Independent 24 May 1974.

Kelly, Eamonn P., 'A bog boat from Derryco', *Kerry Archaeological and Historical Society Journal* 14 (1981).

Kennelly, James P., *The Kerry Way: the History of Kerry Group 1972-2000* (Dublin 2001).

Kerryman 22 September 1935; 4 March 1977; 18, 25 May, 8 June 1979; 16 September 1983; 20 September 1985; 25 September 2003.

Kissane David, *Wings on Their Feet. A Story of Kerry B.L.E. 1967-1998* (Tralee 1998).

Listowel and the GAA 1885-1985 (jointly edited, Tralee, 1985).

Listowel Homecoming: July 31 – August 3, 1992 (Listowel, Canada, 1992).

Listowel Urban District Council: local election results 1899-1999

(Listowel 1999).

Listowel Writers' Week: *Programmes* 1971-2003.

Molyneux, John (ed.), *Clár-cuimhne 1898-1960, Páirc na h-Imeartha, Lios Tuathail* (Tralee 1960).

Molyneux, John, *Lios Tuathail: Páirc Mhic Shíthigh* (Tralee 1981).

O'Brien, Colm, 'The Listowel Singers', *An Ríocht*, 1999.

O'Flaherty, John, *Listowel Races – 1858-1991, a History* (Listowel 1992).

Ó Sé, Páidí, *Páidí*, (Dublin 2001).

Redmond, Markus, 'A survey of the promontory forts of the Kerry peninsulas', *Kerry Archaeological and Historical Society Journal* 28 (1995).

Relihan, Nora, 'Writers' Week in Listowel', *An Ríocht* 2003.

Roche, David, *Local Government in Ireland* (Dublin 1982).

Ryan, Michael, 'A gold box from Ballinclemesig', *Kerry Archaeological and Historical Society Journal* 14 (1981).

St Michael's College, Listowel 1879-1979 (Listowel 1979).

Sunday Tribune 29 June 2003.

Twohig, Dermot C., 'Excavation at Dromkeen East, Causeway', *Kerry Archaeological and Historical Society Journal* 7 (1974).

Twohig, Dermot C., 'Excavation of a Fulacht Fiadh at Dromkeen East, Causeway', *Kerry Archaeological and Historical Society Journal* 10 (1977).

Webb, J.J., *Municipal Government in Ireland: Medieval and Modern* (Dublin 1918).

C
PERSONS

Adams, Peter, 'Shelbourne' Cahirdown, Listowel, County Kerry.

Ahern, Fr Patrick, The Presbytery, Castle Street, Tralee,

County Kerry.

Bracken, Sr Consolata, Presentation Convent, Listowel, County Kerry.

Bunyan, John, 11 Cherrytree Drive, Listowel, County Kerry.

Carmody, Vincent, 25 Patrick Street, Listowel, County Kerry.

Casey, Patrick, Listal Ltd., Listowel, County Kerry.

Daly, Brendan, 13 William Street, Listowel, County Kerry.

Dowling, Michael, Derry, Listowel, County Kerry.

Finucane, Michael, Quay Street, Ballylongford, County Kerry.

Gaine, Michael, Community College, Listowel, County Kerry.

Hartnett, John, Dromclough, Listowel, County Kerry.

Guerin, Michael, Clieveragh, Listowel, County Kerry.

Hannon, Daniel, 29 The Square, Listowel, County Kerry.

Hayes, Frank, Kerry Group plc, Prince's Street, Tralee, County Kerry.

Hayes, Fr George, Bishop's House, Killarney, County Kerry.

Hegarty, Martina, 'An Tóchar', Causeway Education Centre, Causeway, County Kerry.

Horgan, Canon Patrick J., Rathmore, County Kerry.

Leahy, Gerard, 5 Main Street, Listowel, County Kerry.

Linnane, Canon James, The Presbytery, Listowel, County Kerry.

Lynch, Noel, Carrigafoyle, Ballylongford, County Kerry.

McAuliffe, John, 3 Hollytree Drive, Listowel, County Kerry.

McAuliffe, Noreen, The Village, Lixnaw, County Kerry.

McAuliffe, Xavier, Spectra Photo, Clieveragh Industrial Estate, Listowel, County Kerry.

McCarthy, Seán, Community College, Listowel, County Kerry.

McGillicuddy, Mary, Comprehensive School, Tarbert, Listowel, County Kerry.

McKenna, Jack, Greenville, Listowel, County Kerry.

Molyneux, John, 79 Charles Street, Listowel, County Kerry.

Moore, Fr Patrick, The Presbytery, Irremore, Listowel, County Kerry.

Mulvihill, John, St Michael's College, Listowel, County Kerry.

Murphy Joseph, St John's Theatre and Arts Centre, Listowel, County Kerry.

Nolan, Chriss, 'Grenagh', Fossa, Killarney, County Kerry.

O'Carroll, Michael, Main Street, Ballylongford, County Kerry.

O'Donnell, Michelle, Blue Umbrella Gallery, 22 Church Street, Listowel, County Kerry.

O'Keeffe, Gertie, Ballygrennan, Listowel, County Kerry.

O'Neill, Oliver, Cahirdown, Listowel, County Kerry.

O'Shea, Justine, Carrig Road, Ballylongford, County Kerry.

O'Sullivan, Modeleine, Dromin Upper, Listowel, County Kerry.

O'Sullivan, Patrick, 'Oakdene', Cahirdown, Listowel, County Kerry.

O'Reilly, Elizabeth, 'Mount Rivers', Listowel, County Kerry.

Quinlan, Seán, 'Beenduff', Ballyduff, Tralee, County Kerry.

Randles, Sr Eileen, 5 Greenville Road, Blackrock, County Dublin.

Scanlon, Dominic, Dromin, Listowel, County Kerry.

Trant, Cara, The Kerry Literary and Cultural Centre, 24 The Square, Listowel, County Kerry.

Uí Chonchúir, Máire, 'Gleann na Smól', Ballyouneen, Lisselton, County Kerry.

Walsh, William, 'Lisheen', Greenville Road, Listowel, County Kerry.

Wixted, William, Woodford, Listowel, County Kerry.

INDEX